Creating Safe and Sacred Places

Identifying, Preventing, and Healing Sexual Abuse

For all victims of sexual abuse, most especially the survivors of clerical sexual abuse. We honor you who have been harmed. Your lives, your stories, and your pain are not forgotten.

Creating Safe and Sacred Places

Identifying, Preventing, and Healing Sexual Abuse

Gerard J. McGlone, SJ, PhD, and Mary Shrader
with Laurie Delgatto

Saint Mary's Press
Winona, Minnesota

 Genuine recycled paper with 10% post-consumer waste. Printed with soy-based ink. 50779

The publishing team included Laurie Delgatto, development editor; Barbara Murray, contributing editor; Mary Koehler, permissions editor; Mary M. Bambenek, development assistant; Brooke E. Saron, copy editor; Lynn Riska, production editor and typesetter; Andy Palmer, art director; Kimberly K. Sonnek, designer; cover photo © Koji Kitagawa/SuperStock; manufacturing coordinated by the production services department of Saint Mary's Press.

The acknowledgments continue on page 157.

Printed in the United States of America

Printing: 9 8 7 6 5 4 3 2 1

Year: 2011 10 09 08 07 06 05 04 03

ISBN 0-88489-809-1

Library of Congress Cataloging-in-Publication Data

McGlone, Gerard J.
Creating safe and sacred places: identifying, preventing, and healing sexual abuse / Gerard J. McGlone and Mary Shrader with Laurie Delgatto.
p. cm.
Includes bibliographical references.
ISBN 0-88489-809-1 (pbk.)
1. Child sexual abuse by clergy. 2. Catholic Church—Clergy—Sexual behavior. 3. Sex—Religious aspects—Catholic Church. I. Shrader, Mary. II. Delgatto, Laurie. III. Title.
BX1912.9.M34 2003
261.8'3272'088282—dc22

2003015367

Author's Acknowledgments

In loving memory of my parents, Mary and Steve, and my sister, Kathy.

To my family and friends, my family members who have survived sexual abuse; my sojourners who were clients, who were victims and survivors, who were perpetrators; my professors and mentors; my many benefactors; my community at Saint James Catholic Church; and my Jesuit superiors and companions. Each of you has taught me, changed me, supported me, and challenged me to go beyond the ordinary and status quo, to seek that which is "the more" in God's glory and labors.

I want to acknowledge in a special way my coauthors, Mary Shrader and Laurie Delgatto. It is a great source of pride to call each of you both colleague and coauthor. You have made this difficult task a true source of serenity in an arduous effort.

Gerard J. McGlone, SJ, PhD

In appreciation of the parents, young adults, staff, volunteers, and youth who choose to work to keep all young people safe, in light of and in spite of the current events surrounding the issues of sexual abuse in the Church.

For my family, mentors, and teachers who planned and prepared to keep me safe.

This book is written with the hope that those who need to read it will.

Mary Shrader

With deep admiration, respect, and love to Carol and Steve LaBonte for loving me like one of your own. And to John, for your amazing courage.

To Lisa and Joe Correia; Mike and Cher Delgatto; Melissa and Aaron Ketchand; Mitzi, Doug, and Karen Stafford; and all those who listened and believed me when others would not. And for Jake, who took the time to understand. I am so thankful to have each of you walking this journey of healing with me.

Laurie Delgatto

Collectively we wish to express appreciation to the following people:

- Barbara Murray, for her thorough, careful, and pastoral review of this manuscript.
- Maureen Provencher, the author of session 7, "A Listening Session for Young People," which was originally published on the clergy sexual abuse section of the Saint Mary's Press Walking with Teens in Hope Web site (*www.smp.org/tragedy*).

Contents

Foreword *9*

Preface *11*

Introduction *14*

Part A
Understanding Sexual Abuse

Chapter 1: Sexual Abuse: An Overview *23*
- Sexual Abuse Defined *23*
  - Types of Abuse *24*
  - Stages of Abuse *25*
- The Abuser *26*
  - Types of Offenders *27*
  - Warning Signs of a Sexual Predator *28*
- Healthy Sexual Development *28*
- Signs of Sexual Abuse *29*
- Cyber Sex and Abuse *31*
- Long-Term Effects of Sexual Abuse *32*

Chapter 2: Sexual Abuse and the Church *34*
- Understanding the Priest Offender *34*
  - Prevalence and Incidence *35*
- Catholic Context *36*
  - Priesthood's Historical and Theological Background *36*
  - Celibacy and the Priesthood *37*
  - Psychosexual Understanding *38*
- Secrecy and the Church *38*
  - The Church Responds *40*
- Effects of Clerical Sexual Abuse *41*

Chapter 3: Surviving Sexual Abuse *43*
- One Survivor's Story *43*

Part B
Training, Education, and Listening Sessions

Session 1: A Session for Ministry Leaders and Volunteers 51

Session 2: A Session for Ministry Leaders and Volunteers 64

Session 3: A Session for Parents and Guardians 76

Session 4: A Session for Parents and Guardians 89

Session 5: A Session for Young People 98

Session 6: A Session for Young People 111

Session 7: A Listening Session for Young People 119

Session 8: An Intergenerational Session 126

Part C
Resources for Parish and School Staff

Considerations in Ministry Planning 139

Sample Parish Statement for Those Working with Young People 140

Sample Code of Conduct 142

Questions (and Commentary) for Screening Volunteers Who Work with Young People 145

Recommended Resources 147
- Organizations and Web Sites 147
- Educational and Training Videos 150
- Print Resources 151

A Prayer Service of Reconciliation and Rededication 152
- Setting the Prayer Environment 152
- Leadership Roles 152
- Preparation 153
- Procedure 154

Acknowledgments 157

Endnotes Cited in Quotations from the *Catechism of the Catholic Church,* Second Edition 159

Foreword

> For just and unjust a place at the table,
> abuser, abused with need to forgive,
> in anger, in hurt, a mindset of mercy,
> for just and unjust, a new way to live . . .
>
> And God will delight
> when we are creators of justice and joy.
>
> (Shirley Erena Murray, in *A Place at the Table*)

Like most youth ministry professionals, I have been horrified by the recent and ongoing headlines and reports about Church leaders who have sexually abused young people. I have listened to and felt the pain of many abuse victims. There have been too many secrets for too many years. **No secret is a good one.** *Creating Safe and Sacred Places* is an effort to give voice to the secrets of sexual abuse.

As pastoral caretakers of our young people, we have not only a responsibility but also an obligation to ensure that all young people are safe and loved, not only in our churches but also in our schools, homes, and communities. Unfortunately the Church has sometimes fallen short in conveying that message.

As ministers we all know that awareness and understanding is the key to prevention. That is why the publication of this resource manual is so important. We must educate and inform if we are to make any effort to ensure that our young people, *all* young people, are safe and treated with the sacredness God intends.

It is my hope, and our challenge, that each of us comes to understand the need and call to work fervently and diligently to rid all churches, schools, homes, and communities of the sin of sexual abuse. Only then will God delight.

Laurie Delgatto

Preface

As I write this preface, I am well aware of the recent developments in our Church with regard to problems of sexual abuse. Like most, I have been rather stunned and shell-shocked by the revelations and actions of bishops, superiors, fellow priests, and religious. I have been studying, treating, and researching this problem—from the perspective of both the victims and the perpetrators—for almost twelve years, and still I am left amazed and quite perplexed. Particularly troublesome, if not tragic, have been the actions of some in the hierarchy of the Church. How sad and heinous those actions seem in light of all that has happened.

The writing of this manual comes at a critical time in the history of the Catholic Church and all faith-based communities in the United States. The United States Conference of Catholic Bishops acknowledges its role in the enormous and tragic problem of sexual abuse in "Preamble to the Charter for the Protection of Children" (2002). The document notes that in the past the secrecy with which sexual abuse was handled by Church leadership enabled more abuse to occur and was the primary reason for the failure of healing and prevention. It is hoped that this manual breaks down part of this long-standing defense and enables dialogue, education, and, more importantly, healing and prevention to be realized. The issue of sexual abuse is complicated. Add secrecy and cover-up, and the issue becomes even more complex. Yet the subject of sexual abuse must be brought into the open, understood more fully, and discussed more intentionally with all members of our parish and school communities. This manual provides a starting point for such conversation and education. *Creating Safe and Sacred Places* was written with the intent to increase, in parish and school communities, awareness, understanding, skills, and resources in addressing and responding to sexual abuse. You will want to use this resource to gather people for education, prayer, discussion, and action. Those who use this manual should see it as both a prevention resource as well as a pastoral response and a plan to deal with the pain and hurt uncovered by the current crisis. The manual will not answer all questions about the current crisis and certainly is not viewed as "the resource" to rid the Church of abuse. Its intent is to offer both a psychological and a pastoral approach to assist faith-based communities in protecting young people.

The Catholic Church has begun to understand more fully that the abuse of any person—young or old—demands sincere and caring responses that echo the inspiration of the Second Vatican Council to effectively and alertly read the signs of the time. *Creating Safe and Sacred Places* is a response in that tradition.

Gerard J. McGlone, SJ, PhD

In my work in youth ministry, the influence of media, the teachings of the Church, and the simple attention span of a teenager at a Church gathering have challenged me. I have been limited by budgets and time and people-power. Interestingly these same challenges have been catalysts. The issues that have limited me most have actually inspired me to create beyond what I knew and had readily available at my fingertips.

A minister's work demands planning, programming, and educating across a long and wide spectrum of topics: everything from social skills and relationships to service in the community and social justice teaching, from learning prayers to learning how to pray, from Church history and faith stories to present-day leaders and current events, from birth and Baptism to death and eternity. But recently no subject has become more urgent than the topic of sexual abuse in the Church.

Fortunately, in an age of technological advances and widely spread resources, we have more information available to us than we have ever had in the history of the world. But the information age will not save our children. Technology will not hold our children exempt from harm or danger. Not even Church doctrine can magically make all the pain of past offenses go away. So where is the hope?

The hope lies in knowing that the information, the teaching, and the technology can be our allies. The key to prevention is education.

The advances in technology, along with the widespread comprehension of Church teaching, will advance all young people into an age of awareness. Our hope is in believing in the power of community and trusting in the grace of God. Our hope is in seeing the pain of abuse and trusting in the goodness of God's healing.

My hope is that you will view the sessions in this manual as entry points into a broader effort to prevent sexual abuse in your community. When you gather with others to discuss the issues surrounding sexual abuse, you will leave with a reason and the means to create a safe and sacred place for children.

Some participants may leave with feelings of discomfort and disgust. So be it. Sexual abuse of children is disgusting. Some may leave feeling empowered. So be it. Sexual abuse requires our response. Each of us has the opportunity and the responsibility to develop concrete solutions. Some participants may leave feeling hopeless. So be it. God can and does transform hopelessness into hope with the gift of awareness. Some may leave full of ideas and helpful hints. So be it. Allow them the time to put their learnings into perspective and to experiment with being realistic and reasonable.

I encourage you to allow yourself to imagine the incredible opportunities that tackling the issues of sexual abuse might have for you and your faith community. Believe in the power of that opportunity and God's infinite grace. Our children deserve our best.

Mary Shrader

INTRODUCTION

Any initiation of a discussion about sexual abuse will lead to many questions and concerns that a pastoral minister, teacher, or administrator must be prepared to address both individually and communally. This resource presents you, the user, with an important but clear responsibility to respond to such questions and issues ethically, directly, and sensitively.

We suggest that you spend time reflecting on the thoughts and feelings evoked within you when you hear about sexual abuse. Although self-reflection is encouraged and necessary, you need not and *should not* attempt to address this issue on your own. Remember, a communal problem requires a communal response. Initiate discussion and a time for processing with the entire pastoral team. A more informed and educated staff will produce a more informed and educated community. You must be adequately prepared and able to listen to what the members of your community (young and old) have to say about this difficult topic. The best prevention and educational programs are collaborative in their conception and in their implementation.

Teachers, catechists, youth ministers, and pastoral associates must start talking about sexual abuse and the ways to prevent it. Parents need to have open, constructive dialogue with their children. Again, it is important to remember that a communal problem requires a communal response. *Creating Safe and Sacred Places* is designed as a collaborative approach that involves every member of a parish or school staff, and *all* members of a community. We discourage the use of this manual in any other way than the multidimensional manner recommended in the pages that follow.

Preparing for Safe and Sacred Places

Some experts predict the presence of at least one abuser and one victim of abuse anytime there is a gathering focusing on this topic. Someone in your community might be experiencing abuse of some kind, whether physical or sexual, or it may be a part of someone's past. Should you be approached by either a victim or an offender, you will want to be sure you can respond pastorally and quickly. Ask yourself these questions:

- What will I do, or what will my team do, if approached by a potential abuse victim or offender?
- What therapeutic and legal resources are available?
- How prepared am I, and how prepared is my team, to intervene?
- What do the county, state, and diocese require in regard to reporting alleged abuse?

You will want to seek answers to all these questions before initiating any educational or pastoral approaches or programs with the community.

Policies and Procedures

Prior to implementing the sessions found in this manual, your parish or school community will need to establish clear policies and procedures for dealing with and responding to sexual abuse. You will want to check with your local diocesan representative for already established diocesan policies and requirements. Should your diocese not have established guidelines, you will want to be sure that a parish or school policy includes the following items:

- a statement clearly indicating conduct considered unacceptable, unethical, and illegal by your community, the diocese, the Roman Catholic Church, and county and state civil authorities
- clearly determined procedures for community members to file a complaint (including the designation of a specific person within the community to whom a complaint can be made)
- a description of the employment application process for all employees and ministry volunteers who work with children or youth

The United States Conference of Catholic Bishops suggests a number of principles to follow in dealing with accusations of sexual abuse:

- Respond promptly to all allegations of abuse where there is reasonable belief that abuse has occurred.
- If such an allegation is supported by sufficient evidence, relieve the alleged offender promptly of his ministerial duties and refer him for appropriate medical evaluation and intervention.
- Comply with the obligations of civil law as regards reporting of the incident and cooperating with the investigation.
- Reach out to the victims and their families and communicate sincere commitment to their spiritual and emotional well-being.
- Within the confines of respect for privacy of the individuals involved, deal as openly as possible with the members of the community.

("The Five Principles to Follow in Dealing with Accusations of Sexual Abuse," at *www.usccb.org/comm/kit4.htm*)

Parish Guidelines and Code of Conduct

The following are suggested guidelines for all adults working with children and young people. Again, we recommend that you contact your local diocesan representative to ensure that guidelines set by the diocese are incorporated into any parish or school policy.

- At least two adults must always be present for events involving children or young people.
- Release children only to a parent or guardian.
- Always obtain parental permission, including a signed medical treatment form, before taking children or youth off school or church premises.
- Only qualified, licensed, and insured drivers may transport children to and from parish- or school-sponsored events.
- Obtain written parental approval for any young person to participate in athletic events or any other activity that involves potential risk.

A sample code of conduct is included in part C of this manual.

Session Preparation

Honesty

It is your responsibility to be candid and honest from the onset. Those participating in any of the sessions provided in this manual or discussions initiated by community leaders must be told from the start that you have a legal and ethical responsibility to report any alleged abuse, whether it is sexual or physical. Please know that research indicates that physical abuse or neglect might occur much more frequently than people assume. Anticipate this! Consider posting or restating diocesan policies and state laws regarding sexual abuse. Some faith-based communities require participants to sign a statement acknowledging their awareness of the legal and ethical responsibility prior to participating in any discussion of the topic. A sample parish statement is in part C of this manual.

Access to Professional Assistance

An issue such as sexual abuse or domestic violence requires a trained and competent psychological and pastoral counselor. We cannot stress enough the importance of having a professionally trained therapist on hand or readily accessible as you are implementing the programming in this manual. You are not expected to be an expert on these issues. It is important to know your own limitations and those of the staff or program team. Most states and cities have child protection services or agencies with a toll-free telephone number as well as an emergency number to call if abuse of any sort is suspected. It is important to know the names and telephone numbers of such agencies and to have the information readily available for all the participants. A listing of nationally based organizations that offer support and connections to local contacts is in part C of this manual.

Know the Law

Know and abide by the state and county laws as well as your diocesan policy regarding the reporting of alleged abuse. Many states now require anyone who works with young people to report alleged abuse; some require reporting in a timely fashion. Know how soon you are required to report as well as the content of that report.

Consider working with local police and county agencies as you begin to implement the programming in this manual. Initiate conversations and discuss ways those agencies can be involved in the education of your community. The United States Conference of Catholic Bishops (USCCB) has made it clear that all Roman Catholic church and school communities must obey local and county laws regarding sexual abuse. Information on how to obtain copies of the USCCB documents and statements regarding sexual abuse is in part C of this manual.

Conducting the Sessions

Only experienced, skilled, nonjudgmental leaders who can deal responsibly and in a pastorally sensitive manner should lead and conduct the sessions provided in this manual. Working in pairs as facilitators (cofacilitation) is highly recommended. A parish staff member working side-by-side with a professional counselor or social worker from the community is optimal. Creating a supportive, safe, comfortable, and respectful environment in which all participants can risk being vulnerable is a necessity. Session facilitators must be familiar with the session content before conducting any gathering of community members.

There is great potential for authentic and honest sharing for all session participants. At times you will need to acknowledge that some of the information you will be providing may make some participants uncomfortable. Therefore it is essential that participants know they should speak only when they are comfortable doing so.

Consider inviting the participants to discuss and agree upon guidelines for participation and sharing. Engage participants in discussing the positive effects of respect and confidentiality and the destructive effects of sarcasm, judgment calls, and put-downs. You will want to remind the participants of these guidelines each time you gather.

Strategies for Implementation

Consider the following ideas for implementing and integrating the materials found in this resource manual within the overall ministerial programming your parish or school offers:

- at the beginning of a new year or school year with teachers and educators
- as a mandatory open session for any parish volunteer, schoolteacher, or ministry volunteer
- on a teacher in-service day
- as a series of sessions addressing family, child, or community safety
- as a chapter or topic of gender issues
- as a regular yearly (or more frequent) session in the religious education curriculum
- as an invitation to the parish or school community to be a child advocate
- in preparation for a school or parish outing or event
- as a portion of training for teen peer leaders
- as part of staff or parish council planning and programming for the year

Consider pairing the sessions in this manual with presentations offered by:

- a diocesan representative, legal consultant, social worker, or therapist on the prevention of child abuse
- a staff member from the local rape crisis center, abuse shelter, or other local agency that provides prevention and intervention services in the community

- parents who can speak on behalf of all parents about an experience of protecting their children
- a survivor or advocate for sexual abuse victims

Ongoing Prevention and Education

Your community can do several things to inform, prevent, and respond to sexual abuse. The following are essential strategies you will want to incorporate into parish- or school-wide ministries:

- All young people need to know that their bodies are sacred. Talk openly about safe versus unsafe touch.
- Remember, most offenders will be known by the potential victim.
- All young people need to develop good and solid relationships with peers, parents, and significant adults whom they can trust.
- Background checks and supervision are simply unavoidable for any adult volunteer or paid employee. Be clear about the procedures and processes required by your diocese.
- Proper boundaries need to be talked about and respected within staffs and parish communities.
- Nothing is more sacred than communication, and nothing is more preventative! Research points to communication as key to prevention. Good, nonjudgmental communication assumes mutual respect, regardless of any information that a child or young person may share.
- Open discussion about sexual matters, although uncomfortable, needs to be pursued and encouraged, especially within families.
- Do not assume anything about anyone.

Part A

UNDERSTANDING SEXUAL ABUSE

Chapter 1

SEXUAL ABUSE: AN OVERVIEW

Prevention begins with education and information exchange and must continue with all members of the family, school community, and faith-based community being aware and agreeing that normative sexuality should include the basic premise that **no child is to be harmed.** This principle may seem obvious, but the more we speak of basic values, the more we can realize our hope of stopping child abuse altogether.

Sexual Abuse Defined

> Sexual abuse of a minor includes sexual molestation or sexual exploitation of a minor and other behavior by which an adult uses a minor as an object of sexual gratification. Sexual abuse has been defined by different civil authorities in various ways, and these norms do not adopt any particular definition provided in civil law. Rather, the transgressions in question relate to obligations arising from divine commands regarding human sexual interaction as conveyed by the sixth commandment of the Decalogue. Thus, the norm to be considered in assessing an allegation of sexual abuse of a minor is whether conduct or interaction with a minor qualifies as an external, objectively grave violation of the sixth commandment. (USCCB, *Canonical Delicts Involving Sexual Misconduct and Dismissal from the Clerical State,* 1995, p. 6.) [This may not be a

> complete act of sexual intercourse.] Nor, to be objectively grave, does it need to involve force, physical contact, or a discernible harmful outcome. (USCCB, "Essential Norms for Diocesan/Eparchial Policies Dealing with Allegations of Sexual Abuse of Minors by Priests or Deacons")

The bishops' definition provides us with more than just a common language; it provides us with a moral imperative. The imagery in the definition and the particular point the bishops make are that any form of violence committed against a child or minor goes against the most basic commandments given to Moses long ago. Our moral code and standard must be honored and respected, especially with regard to sexual abuse, because any harm against "one of these little ones" is a crime against God and God's commands.

Types of Abuse

Physical abuse in the United States is a staggering problem. Domestic violence research indicates that corporal punishment is the primary way children experience trauma in our society. Violence against children happens in various forms. Sexual abuse, one form of violence against children, can itself take on various forms. It can involve sexual intercourse, fondling under or over the clothes, or sexual exploitation where no direct physical action is perpetrated upon the child but where the child is in the presence of an offender who is clearly becoming sexually aroused by the child's presence. An example of this sexual exploitation is an offender's exposing a child to pornography while watching to see what the child does in response. Another example is an offender's taking photos of a naked child for personal sexual stimulation.

Some other common forms of sexual abuse include:

- sexual penetration, anally and vaginally
- oral sex
- bondage
- observing others engaging in sexual acts

> Statistics show that child sexual abuse occurs at an alarming rate. At least one in three to five girls and one in seven to ten boys will be sexually abused at some point in their childhood. It is hard to take in this cold hard fact. It means that if you attend a class or concert of 100 people, between 10 and 20 of those in the room were sexually abused as a child. *(www.stopitnow.org)*

Sexual abuse of a child is most often committed by an offender who knows the victim. Abuse by strangers is rare. Sexual abuse often occurs in familiar places such as the family home. "In 90 percent of child sexual abuse cases, the child knows and trusts the person who commits the abuse" (Finkelhor, 1994). "Abusers are fathers, mothers, stepparents, grandparents, and other family members (uncles, aunts, cousins). They're neighbors, babysitters, religious leaders, teachers, coaches, or anyone else who has close contact with our children" (Rogers and Tremain, 1984). "In 90 percent of child sexual abuse cases, the offenders are male" (Florida Center for Parent Involvement, "Sexual Abuse and Young Children").

Stages of Abuse

Sexual abuse usually occurs in stages. An offender normally "grooms" the victim, recruiting him or her through good observation and knowledge. An offender might groom his or her victim by giving gifts, taking the victim on special trips, or spending special time with the victim. This seduction of sorts sets up the offense, and then the offender molests or offends the child. Depending on the coercion and satisfaction achieved, the offender might break off the relationship and move on to a new victim. Understanding this process is one of the first ways that children can become better at stopping abuse before it occurs. If a child ever feels weird or uncomfortable about an adult, or if parents sense a lack of comfortableness in their child, they must trust their instincts!

Some factors that contribute to the various stages of abuse include these:

- The sexual contact arises from a relationship involving immense trust on the part of the child and parents.
- In the case of clerical sexual abuse, the child is extraordinarily vulnerable in that he or she sees the priest as an agent of God.
- Because an affectionate relationship often precedes the sexual contact, the child feels that he or she has a very special relationship with the abuser.
- The child feels an incredible sense of helplessness. Most abused children feel either responsible for the abuse's occurring or so powerless that they think they cannot disclose the abuse to their parents or to anyone else.
- Such secrecy surrounds the abuse that disclosure is inhibited. The abuser may even make threats to keep the child silent, allowing the abuser to continue violating the child.
- Criminal and civil complaints indicate that alcohol is a major agent in the seduction process. The offender introduces alcohol to the dynamics of the relationship so that the sexual encounters are less stressful for both the abuser and the victim.

To initiate any training, education, or discussion regarding sexual abuse, you must use a common language and a common vocabulary. Equally important is the need for all Church leaders to understand the full scope of the kind of abuse an innocent child might endure under the power and influence of an adult offender. One of the most common bits of advice that children need to hear is that *they* are the only ones who determine what is safe and sacred in their world. You must encourage all children to trust their instincts, and you must provide safe ways and opportunities for young people to talk about their feelings.

The Abuser

Consider these commonly held myths about sexual abuse offenders and the facts that disprove these myths:

- **Myth.** Most sexual offenders are strangers.
  - **Fact.** Most sexual assaults are committed by someone familiar to the victim or the victim's family, regardless of whether the victim is a child or an adult.
- **Myth.** The majority of sexual offenders are caught, convicted, and sentenced to prison.
  - **Fact.** Only a fraction of those who commit sexual assault are apprehended and convicted for their crimes. Most convicted sex offenders are eventually released into the community under probation or parole supervision.
- **Myth.** All offenders will offend again.
  - **Fact.** Reconviction data suggest that this is not the case. Re-offense rates vary among different types of sex offenders and are related to specific characteristics of the offender and the offense.
- **Myth.** Sexual offense rates are higher than ever and continue to climb.
  - **Fact.** Despite the increase in publicity about sexual crimes, the actual rate of reported sexual assault has decreased slightly in recent years.
- **Myth.** All offenders are male.
  - **Fact.** The vast majority of sex offenders are male, but females also commit sexual crimes.
- **Myth.** Sex offenders commit sexual crimes because they are under the influence of alcohol.
  - **Fact.** It is unlikely that an individual who otherwise would not commit a sexual assault would do so as a direct result of excessive drinking.
- **Myth.** Children who are sexually assaulted will sexually assault others when they grow up.
  - **Fact.** Most sex offenders were not sexually assaulted as children, and most adults who were sexually assaulted as children do not sexually assault others.

- **Myth.** Youths do not commit sex offenses.
  - **Fact.** Adolescents are responsible for a significant number of rape and child molestation cases each year.
- **Myth.** Juvenile sex offenders typically are victims of child sexual abuse and grow up to be adult sex offenders.
  - **Fact.** Multiple factors, not just sexual victimization as a child, are associated with the development of sexually offending behavior in youth.

(Adapted from "Myths and Facts About Sex Offenders," at *www.csom.org*)

Perpetrators of sexual abuse most often know their victims. Offenders cross every socio-economic classification, every race, every sexual orientation, and every educational, ethnic, or cultural description. The classic breakdown most often used is the exclusive offender, the one who is attracted to just children, versus the nonexclusive offender, the person who is attracted to adults and children. The most common offender is a married, heterosexual, white, respected male.

Contrary to the impression one may get from the media, offenders are also found in every religious background. Over the years survivors have come forward about their abuse from most, if not all, the established mainline religious denominations, including Anglican, Assembly of God, Baptists, Baptist Missionary, Buddhist, Byzantine Rite, Christian Fellowship, Christian Science, Church of God, Conservative Fundamentalist, Eastern Orthodox, Evangelical Lutheran Church of America (ELCA), Episcopal, Evangelical, Greek Orthodox, Jehovah's Witnesses, Jewish, Liberal Church of God, Methodist, Mormon, Nondenominational, Lutheran Church Missouri Synod (LCMS), Presbyterian, Roman Catholic, and Unitarian.

Types of Offenders

- **Opportunist.** An opportunistic offender seeks out children regularly until caught.
- **Experimenter.** This type of offender abuses as part of sexual exploration.
- **Inadequate and opportunistic.** This type of offender is mentally inadequate or has a stunted mental development.
- **Pedophile.** A pedophile has no sexual interest in adults and is sexually attracted to only prepubescent children, under the age of thirteen.
- **Ephebophile.** An ephebophile is sexually attracted to only postpubescent children, adolescents between the ages of fourteen and eighteen.
- **Pederast.** This type of offender engages in anal intercourse with boys under the age of eighteen.

- **Nonexclusive.** This type of offender is married or in a relationship with another adult but clearly desires children sexually and uses every opportunity to find situations where sexual contact with a child can happen.
- **Exclusive offender.** This type of offender is attracted only to children.
- **Sex offender.** A sex offender is an individual who is either an ephebophile or a pedophile.

Warning Signs of a Sexual Predator

The following list describes some signs that a person might be a sexual predator:

- insists on hugging, touching, kissing, tickling, wrestling with, or holding a child even when the child does not want this affection
- is overly interested in the sexuality of a particular child or teen (e.g., talks repeatedly about a child's developing body or interferes with normal teen dating)
- manages to get time alone or insists on time alone with a child with no interruptions, such as weekend sleepovers, vacations, or camping trips
- spends most of his or her spare time with children or teens and has little interest in spending time with someone his or her own age
- regularly offers to baby-sit or takes children on outings alone
- buys children and teens expensive gifts or gives them money for no apparent reason
- frequently walks in on children or teens in the bathroom
- allows children or teens to consistently get away with inappropriate behaviors

Healthy Sexual Development

It is crucial for you to both understand and appreciate normal adolescent development before looking at what might be abnormal reactions to sexual experiences and sexual abuse. Parents and teachers commonly observe odd and seemingly weird developments in once "happy and normal" children. Teens and preteens can experience strange biological changes that are often coupled with unusual physical changes. These changes in liking and disliking what the body feels and looks like are often accompanied by sudden and dramatic mood fluctuations that seem to have little foundation in everyday events and perceptions. Children of this age-group are often at odds with authority in some way because they see a substantial need to reconfigure their world and the meanings within their world. Risk-taking behavior is often characteristic of teens and preteens not only because of age-appropriate questioning but also because they don't have developmental capacities to predict long-term effects and are testing limits as a way to see whom they can trust. The result is often self-doubts, valid fears, persistent conflicts, and ruminative preoccupations. Additionally some young people struggle to adjust to changing social relationships and a changing social environment.

Now add sex to this picture. If children have been given inaccurate or no information about sex, this void becomes the foundation upon which their adaptive, developmentally appropriate curiosity will be based. A child who has gone through previous developmental phases well, with proper environmental and familial supports and with adequate coping skills, will have the best chance to progress—as best as can be expected—through the developmental stage called adolescence.

It is essential to be aware of and discuss with young people what is a *normal* exploration of sexuality, what might be called age specific, and what is not normal. Sometimes curiosity—thigh rubbing, some forms of exhibitionism (e.g., streaking), peeking while others are undressing (voyeurism), exploring body parts—might be part of a "normative" sexual experience for preteens and teens. However, some behaviors seem to be fairly well accepted as abnormal for teens and juveniles, including these:

- placing his or her mouth on a sex part
- asking to engage in sex acts
- masturbating with objects
- imitating intercourse
- making sexual sounds
- French kissing
- undressing other people
- asking to watch explicit television
- viewing pornography on the Internet or on television
- imitating sexual behavior with dolls

This agreed-upon set of behaviors points to the types of activities you must view within the context of a relationship in order to fully distinguish between normal and abnormal, or abusive, interactions. Consensus seems to point to the following five dynamics as significant to consider in making this distinction:

- a significant age difference
- the amount of coercion used or exhibited
- the lack of consent
- the dynamic of inequality
- the degree of force

Signs of Sexual Abuse

The main reason abuse is not reported immediately is that so often it happens in a secluded place. There are often no witnesses. We cannot overstate the importance of understanding these essential aspects. Silence and secrecy are common. Fear, a sense of betrayal, helplessness, a feeling of entrapment, and a feeling of not wanting to cause trouble are all reasons why most victims remain silent. Most often a victim will tell of the abuse years later only because she or he felt too ashamed, too guilty, and somewhat responsible for the abuse at that time it happened. "You wouldn't believe me. You never do." "I was too ashamed, embarrassed, and humiliated." "I thought it was my fault." "I didn't want our family to be embarrassed." "I wanted to protect you." "Dad told me that it would destroy you." "I got an erection." "I thought I could handle it." These are all common reasons that victims give for not reporting their abuse right away.

Children, however, give many signs through their behavior, but parents and other significant adults who care for children (teachers, relatives, coaches, and so forth) commonly overlook changes in behavior. They can have an even more difficult time identifying signs when a victim is a preadolescent or adolescent because of the number of physical, emotional, and spiritual changes that take place during this stage of development.

Some *psychological* markers or red flags for adults to notice include these:

- a child who clearly says, "I just don't want to be around or alone with Uncle X anymore."
- any avoidance that is confusing or of concern
- sudden mood or behavioral shifts, both before and after an encounter with an adult
- hyperactivity
- too much sleep, too little sleep, difficulty sleeping, nightmares, or sleep disturbances
- changes in eating habits (loss of appetite or trouble eating or swallowing)
- fear of previously likable places and people; fear of making friends; fear of situations, such as being in the dark or being alone; startled responses to loud noises or voices; possible paranoia about being watched or chased
- aggressiveness (verbal or physical), defiance, delinquent behavior, excessive risk-taking behaviors
- new words for private body parts
- difficulty at bath time
- regression in behavior (i.e., an older child behaving like a younger child by doing such things as wetting the bed or sucking a thumb)

- depression, withdrawal, isolation, self-mutilation, suicide attempts
- changes in academic performance
- talking about a new older friend
- refusing to talk about a "secret" that she or he has with an adult or older child

Some *physical* markers or red flags for adults to notice include these:

- unexplained bruises, redness, or bleeding from the genitals, anus, or mouth
- unexplained urinary infection or sexually transmitted disease
- frequent headaches, stomachaches, or body aches
- fatigue or feeling overly tired or unmotivated
- heart palpitations or difficulty breathing
- various sexual reactions, from being overly fearful to being promiscuous
- unintended pregnancy at an early age
- in younger children, constant rubbing or irritation of genitalia
- persistent sexual play with other children, themselves, toys, or pets
- displaying sexual knowledge through language or behavior (beyond what is normal for a child's age)
- drug or alcohol problems
- self-destructive behaviors such as scarring arms with razor blades, needles, or cigarettes
- spacing out at odd times

Cyber Sex and Abuse

Now add the computer to the scenario. The advent of the computer has introduced to children an incalculable number of resources that were not available just a decade ago. The computer and the Internet have given people the opportunity to connect with family and peers, no matter the distance, and to quickly access various sources of knowledge. The Internet can be a place for open discussion and exchange of ideas, but it can also be a very dangerous place.

Anonymity and safety have become the hallmarks of this type of cyber activity. The Internet is, therefore, the new playground, basketball court, park, or meeting place for perpetrators. Children who fall victim to cyber sexual predators are often the kinds of kids who appear confused, curious, or isolated. Anonymity is a mask for offenders, but it also gives the victim the illusion of safety.

Victims of cyber sexual abuse are often "groomed" or told how wonderful they are. Often these children have experienced a history of abuse in the home. They are perceived by offenders as someone who won't tell, is curious about sex, and wants attention and affection.

In June 2000, the Crimes Against Children Research Center conducted interviews with a nationally representative sample of 1,501 youth, ages ten to seventeen, who use the Internet regularly. The interviews revealed the following statistics:

- Approximately one in five received a sexual solicitation or approach over the Internet in the last year.
- One in thirty-three received an aggressive sexual solicitation—a solicitor who asked to meet them somewhere, called them on the telephone, or sent them regular mail, money, or gifts.
- In the last year, one in four had an unwanted exposure to pictures of naked people or people having sex.
- One in seventeen was threatened or harassed.
- Approximately one quarter of the young people who reported these incidents were distressed by them.
- Less than 10 percent of sexual solicitations and only 3 percent of unwanted exposure episodes were reported to authorities such as a law-enforcement agency, an Internet service provider, or a hotline.
- About one quarter of the youth who encountered a sexual solicitation or approach told a parent.
- Almost 40 percent of those reporting an unwanted exposure to sexual material told a parent.
- Only 17 percent of youth and approximately 10 percent of parents could name a specific authority (such as the FBI, CyberTipline, or an Internet service provider) to which they could make a report, although more said they had heard of such places.

("Online Victimization," at *www.missingkids.com/missingkids/servlet*)

Long-Term Effects of Sexual Abuse

The long-term effects of sexual abuse have been well researched and known for some time. The full extent of the impact on the victim is determined by several factors, including these:

- the type of abuse
- the victim's relationship to the abuser
- the age of the victim when the abuse took place
- developmental and psychological resources that the young person had at his or her disposal at the time
- the extent of the perpetration and the victim's ability to "make sense of it"
- the family connections, relationships, or dynamics

Each of these factors adds to a portrait of resiliency—the way a child copes with trauma and violence of any sort.

The traumatic sexualization, stigmatization, betrayal, and powerlessness that sexual abuse victims experience are manifested in long-term effects that can become debilitating and life threatening. The long-term effects can include these:

- anger
- fear
- homosexuality issues among males
- helplessness
- isolation and alienation
- loss
- masculinity issues among males
- negative childhood peer relations
- negative images about people
- negative self-image
- problems with sexuality
- self-blame and guilt
- shame and humiliation
- anxiety
- depression
- dissociation
- impaired relationships
- sexual dysfunction
- sleep disturbance
- suicidal thoughts and behaviors
- problems with intimacy
- sexual problems or compulsions
- substance abuse
- symptoms of post-traumatic stress disorder
- attempts to "prove" masculinity or femininity by having multiple sex partners, by sexually victimizing others, or by engaging in dangerous or violent behaviors
- confusion in males about gender and sexual identity
- sense of being inadequate as a man or woman
- sense of lost power, control, and confidence in maleness or femaleness
- homophobia, an irrational fear or intolerance of homosexuality
- fear in men that the sexual abuse has caused or will cause them to become homosexual; fear in women that they will be denied marriage and motherhood

Chapter 2

Sexual Abuse and the Church

Sexual abuse often occurs in relationships between the powerful and the powerless. Clearly a priest is in a position of power in the Church and in the lives of young people. The clear majority of priests are able to relate normally and healthily in such an environment. Others simply cannot.

Understanding the Priest Offender

Sexual abuse of children by members of the Roman Catholic clergy is an enormously complex and tragic problem in today's society. The problem is not specific to the Roman Catholic clergy or Church; it happens in every faith tradition and congregation. Since the early 1980s, many priests and brothers have been labeled pedophiles by the media. Sensationalism, agendas of varied sorts, and intrigue surround most of these stories. Few accounts offer any help in understanding the problem. Scientific terms are used with little regard for their meaning and little care for their importance.

Clerical sexual abuse takes place within a relationship of power and dominance. Clearly some in authority—whether they are cardinals, bishops, priests, rabbis, or ministers—have misused their roles to such an extent that the victims' concept and very experience of the sacred, if not their full reality of it, are sacrificed and, in some cases, destroyed. The experience, harm, and pain of clerical sexual abuse must never escape notice, and the Church's attentiveness will lead to a better understanding of this substantial abuse problem.

Some very important caveats might be helpful. This chapter is one attempt to add clarity to understanding a serious societal, religious, and familial problem. The present clerical sexual abuse situation is so fluid that the current statistics might be outdated by the time this resource is published. The following information is not, nor should it ever be, construed to be a justification for any criminal or immoral behavior of an individual or institution. Unfortunately, in the current atmosphere, some myths might be presented as facts, and some facts might be used for varying agendas on the left and the right.

Prevalence and Incidence

The Center for Applied Research in the Apostolate at Georgetown University estimates the total number of priests in the United States to be about 44,000. It estimates that 37,000 of these priests are diocesan clergy, with the remaining being religious order priests. Reliable statistical figures for sex offenders among the 44,000 Catholic clergymen in the United States are extremely difficult to ascertain. Little is known about sexually offending priests because of many factors, not the least of which has been the Catholic Church's resistance to sponsor and lead research in this area. The June 2002 gathering of the United States Conference of Catholic Bishops, in Dallas, Texas, mandated full reporting of all cases, with details on numbers and percentages related to the occurrence of clerical sexual abuse in every diocese in the United States. The June 2003 gathering, held in Saint Louis, Missouri, seems to have moved this data collection one more step to becoming known and acknowledged. Therefore, any numbers given here refer to detected or admitted rates of abuse, not what might be known as "true" rates of prevalence.

Although some people question the percentages and numbers of clerical abusers, almost no one doubts that the majority of priest offenders are classified as ephebophiles. The inability to clearly distinguish between the two most common types of sexual offenders, the pedophile and the ephebophile, prevents the public and, therefore, most Catholics, from fully understanding the breadth and depth of the problem within the Church.

Catholic Context

To understand the problem of priest sex offenders, we must examine it within its uniquely Catholic context. Three important aspects of the Roman Catholic clergy must be discussed: (1) historical and theological background, (2) celibacy and the priesthood, and (3) psychosexual understanding.

Priesthood's Historical and Theological Background

Throughout its nearly 2,000-year history, the Catholic Church has attempted to fulfill one essential mission: to proclaim Christ Jesus and the Gospel. Within this mission, priests have come to be seen as one essential instrument among many. The ministry of the ordained, particularly of bishops and their coworkers, priests, differs from the ministry of all believers in an essential way. Holy Orders confers on men a sacred power for the service of the faithful, a power that comes to them from Christ through Christ's Church. The authority given them can be traced back to the Apostles, and in the Catholic Church, bishops are considered the successors of the Apostles. In both past and present theology, the priest acts in the person of Christ when he leads the community in sacramental celebrations. These theological roots date back to the Old Testament, in which the sons of Aaron and the descendants of Abraham used priests "appointed on behalf of men in relation to God, to offer gifts and sacrifices for sins"[1] (*Catechism of the Catholic Church [CCC]*, no. 1539). From the perspective of Catholic belief, Christ came into salvation history to end, once and for all, the Hebrew sacrificing. Christ's sacrifice of himself before God's throne is complete in the very person and sacrifice of Christ on the cross. This eucharistic memorial is celebrated at every Mass in the actions of the priest and the community. From this belief it follows logically that the priest unites himself to the sacrifice of Christ, and each member of the community participates through this priestly ministry.

Over time the priest's role became more and more significant within both ecclesiastical and civil structures while the participation of the community diminished. This point is illustrated in the many historical counts of priests who exercised civil authority over towns and territories during the medieval period.

The combination of secular and spiritual power throughout history created both enormous privileges and problems for the priest. Church history shows that the order, or rank, of priest became more significant. Acting *in persona Christi,* "in the person of Christ," the priest functioned in an office and role that could not allow him to be anything but what that office and role dictated. As early as the fifth century, Saint Gregory of Nazianzus put it aptly:

> Who then is the priest? He is the defender of truth, who stands with angels, gives glory to archangels, causes sacrifices to rise to the altar on high, shares Christ's priesthood, refashions creation, restores it in God's image, recreates it for the world on high and, even greater, is divinized and divinizes.[2] (*CCC*, no. 1589)

Saint Gregory put into focus the enormous tasks, expectations, and pressures that the priest faces in his attempt to be similar to this *Alter Christus*, another Christ. "The priest continues the work of redemption on earth"[3] (*CCC*, no. 1589). Theology surrounding the priesthood changed after the Council of Trent in the sixteenth century. The priest's very being was defined as forever changed as a result of being ordained into the "order" of "priest." In this Catholic framework, ordination to the priesthood is such a significant and altering event that even if a priest decides to renounce his duties, he can never technically resign from being a priest. The Church teaches that an "indelible mark" has been placed on his soul. This mark is eternal and forever identifies the ordained as a priest. "He cannot become a layman again in the strict sense,[4] because the character imprinted by ordination is forever" (*CCC*, no. 1583). In being ordained, the priest, as stated in Hebrews 5:6, is considered "a priest forever according to the order of Melchizedek."

Celibacy and the Priesthood

Celibacy has always been part of the priesthood. Just as Christ remained celibate and dedicated his life to the service of his Father and all people, a priest accepts celibacy and consecrates himself totally to serve the mission of the Lord. Just as Christ is totally united to the Church, the priest, through his celibacy, bonds his life to the Church. He is the minister of the sacraments and, especially through the Mass, acts in the person of Christ, offering himself totally to the Lord. Celibacy is not a dogma of faith but a disciplinary law designed to increase the dignity of the priesthood. In the early Church, many married men were chosen for the offices of priest and bishop, but as the supply of single, eligible men became greater, more of them were ordained in preference to the married men.

Celibacy became mandatory in the Western Church during the eleventh century as part of the reforms of Pope Saint Gregory VII. The Church needed to protect its property and rights against the eldest son's medieval hereditary rights. Essentially, mandatory celibacy as a discipline for all priests came into being to address a growing economic and property rights crisis. What was originally considered a gift and a path freely chosen by some priests became a required discipline for all who desire to exercise priestly ministry. Church history is filled with the lived and rich tradition of the spiritual discipline of chastity—to follow Jesus in every way. However, sacred and profane reasons often exist alongside each other.

Psychosexual Understanding

Celibates are sexual creatures. It has been popular in Jesuit nomenclature, tradition, training, and formation for almost five hundred years to use the experience and folklore of Ignatius of Loyola, the Basque founder of the Jesuits, as a model for living celibately. His experience—post-conversion, of course—was, in matters of celibacy, to be like the angels. In other words, to live celibately was not, in the modern sense, an "issue" for Ignatius and was not to be one for his followers.

Celibacy and living a celibate life require more than an exhortation to be like the angels. Healthy sexual development within the clergy requires constant formation, care, and dedication. A priest's sexual and physical development as a person does not stop the minute he vows to live a chaste life. The priest, the faith community, and the institution must bear enormous responsibilities in this regard throughout the priest's life in the Church community.

The role and function of the priest are necessarily different from the role and function of other individuals in the Church and in society. Such a distinction can prevent the priest from establishing relationships that provide intimacy, support, and natural comfort. Some scholars speculate that priests avoid being intimate because of this unique pastoral role and the way other people view them. Others theorize that if a priest becomes intimate, he runs the risk of being sexually active. This tendency is noted time and time again as a deficiency and an inability to relate or, more psychologically, as an inability to sustain relationships that are enduring. This understanding of the priest's distinction is changing in today's Church.

Secrecy and the Church

In the late 1930s, psychiatric research and writing began to acknowledge the harm of adult sexual activity with children. The advent of reporting laws in 1962 highlighted the growing awareness of the severe harm that sexual abuse of children engendered on the child victim.

As early as the 1960s, Catholic bishops and religious superiors attempted to handle some of the more severe cases of sexual misconduct through the use of psychiatry and psychology. This effort grew in size, scope, and sophistication until, by the late 1970s, Catholic treatment centers were on the cutting edge of treatment techniques for

Catholic priests and religious who had acted out sexually with young people.

A 1985 Louisiana case involving an accused priest in the Diocese of Lafayette was unique because, for the first time, evidence of prior knowledge on the part of the bishop was made public. In his groundbreaking book *Lead Us Not into Temptation* (Champaign, IL: University of Illinois Press, 2000), Jason Berry told the story of Fr. Gilbert Gauthe and summoned national attention to the issue while depicting the typical scenario that has been repeated again and again.

Father Gauthe was stationed in a small town in Louisiana. The dynamic young priest was most popular with the older ladies and the youth of the parish. He apparently had few social relationships with men or women his own age but seemed happy with his work, especially his work with young boys. Oddly enough Father Gauthe did not spend a lot of time at any one parish assignment. Later the reason became clear: Father Gauthe had been molesting boys in a variety of settings.

Church officials apparently knew there had been some incidents with young boys, but evidently they misjudged the severity of those encounters. Father Gauthe admitted that he needed help because he had been kissing some of the boys. At the time, Church officials offered him spiritual counseling. That decision, sadly enough, afforded the perpetrator more access to new and different victims.

In time the Church's refusal to protect other victims from this particular man forced formerly devout Catholics to speak out publicly against their Church and its officials. The parents of victims, with the help of media support and attention, finally forced a more public and responsible reaction from the Church. Legal action forced the walls of denial to fall. It also resulted in the media's paying more attention to similar stories and to the scandal of clerical sexual abuse in general. Father Gauthe was finally removed from the priesthood. Children were at long last protected. The financial settlement in just this one case reached into the tens of millions of dollars.

The purpose of the media in such cases is a hotly debated topic. On the one hand, the media's tendency to sensationalize has led to inaccurate portrayals of priests as pedophiles and ephebophiles and to clearly inaccurate reports on the magnitude and size of the problem; on the other hand, subsequent to the initial case of Father Gauthe, many more cases have been discovered and reported by the media only.

Historically, in case after case of sexual abuse, the same scenario seems to be repeated: The perpetration occurs. Years pass. Somehow the secret is broken, evidence comes to light, a victim recalls the abuse, or the priest is caught in a new act of offending. Church officials send the perpetrator away, and legal action by the Church or the families may begin. The victim is silently ignored, or therapy is offered with financial settlement being given for silence to reign over the incident and its details. The victim is usually sent for treatment or given the choice of treatment in some form. Frequently the community of believers, abandoned and confused, is left alone, ignorant, and in the dark about the priest's sudden departure. The picture is often one of secrecy, denial, unexplained scandal, and unspoken absence.

The Church Responds

> The Catholic Church in the United States is in a very grave crisis, perhaps the gravest we have faced. This crisis is not about a lack of faith in God. In fact, those Catholics who live their faith actively day-by-day will tell you that their faith in God is not in jeopardy; it has indeed been tested by this crisis, but it is very much intact. The crisis, in truth, is about a profound loss of confidence by the faithful in our leadership as shepherds, because of our failures in addressing the crime of the sexual abuse of children and young people by priests and Church personnel. What we are facing is not a breakdown in belief, but a rupture in our relationship as Bishops with the faithful. And this breakdown is understandable. We did not go far enough to ensure that every child and minor was safe from sexual abuse. Rightfully, the faithful are questioning why we failed to take the necessary steps. . . .
>
> These are times that cry out for a genuine reconciliation within the Church in our country; not a reconciliation that merely binds a wound so that we can move forward together in some hobbled kind of fashion. What we need is a reconciliation that heals: one that brings us together to address this issue in a way that ensures that it will not happen again; one that begins with a love of the Truth that is Jesus Christ; one that embraces fully and honestly the authentic elements of the Sacrament of Penance as we celebrate it in the Catholic tradition. Only by truthful confession, heartfelt contrition, and firm purpose of amendment can we hope to receive the generous mercy of God and the forgiveness of our brothers and sisters.
>
> ("A Catholic Response to Sexual Abuse: Confession, Contrition, Resolve," at *www.usccb.org/bishops/presidentialaddress.htm*)

Churches and Church officials have been slow to respond but recently have shown greater diligence. Encouraged and compelled by expensive lawsuits, reluctant insurance carriers, and the example of churches and individuals devastated by clerical abuse, as well as a sense of moral commitment and integrity, Church officials are now more willing to remove an abusive priest.

At the June 2002 semi-annual meeting of the United States Conference of Catholic Bishops (USCCB), Church leaders resolved to create national standards and policies for dealing with the devastating pain and sorrow of abuse victims. In addition the bishops established national standards and processes for protecting all children in the future. Finally, the bishops committed to and established national processes for consistently and vigilantly dealing with sexually offending clergy.

> We have thus made a solemn commitment to our people that the priesthood will not be used to harm a child.
>
> We are backing that commitment up with unprecedented means to hold ourselves accountable to our people. A National Office for Child and Youth Protection will report annually on our successes—and failures—in implementing our commitment in all our dioceses. . . .
>
> The Charter for the Protection of Children and Young People is both a commitment and a way for the Catholic people and all our fellow Americans to see that this commitment is being fulfilled.
>
> ("Bishop Gregory Stresses Force of Action on Child Sexual Abuse," at *www.usccb.org/comm/archives/2002/02-113.htm*)

Most bishops and Church officials are now encouraging open conversation about sexual abuse in order to allow the processes of healing and understanding to begin.

Effects of Clerical Sexual Abuse

Priestly perpetration has enormous associations and implications for the victims, especially when those victims are children. The priest represents more than just himself to a child. In the eyes of a child who is abused by a priest, God, Christ, and the Church, as well as the priest, are the abusers. Because children are often taught to see their priest as a man of holiness and righteousness, they logically view their priest as godlike. Thus, if God is viewed as holy, this man of God must be equally holy. Imagine the enormous internal conflict children must experience witnessing parishioners bowing, kneeling, praying, and receiving sacraments from an abuser.

In Catholic theology, the normative understanding of God is that of Father. In this same Church, only a male can be a priest, and a priest is called Father. It seems evident, then, that because God is Father and the priest is called Father and is viewed as godlike by children, the sexual abuse perpetrated can have a shattering and devastating effect. It clearly can affect a child's perception of God, sense of self, and ability to develop intimate relationships with others.

When a Father, God's representative, abuses a child, the shame associated with the abuse tends to keep the child silent about the situation. Those who have broken their silence are often not believed as children or as adults. Abused children often struggle with the thought that they must be very bad for God to have allowed the abuse to happen in the first place. Abused Catholics, as adults, struggle with trusting an institution they were taught contained the fullness of truth and salvation. Developmental delays often can occur in adults who were abused as children, and fears of revictimization prevent many from even entering a church again. To simplify: the priest = the Church; the Church = God; therefore, the priest = God.

Churches are intended to be communities of faith where the inherent worth and dignity of all people are honored and respected, where each person is a child of God and should be held safely in God's care. When abused by a priest, a victim's inherent worth and dignity are disregarded and violated, and the foundations of religious faith are betrayed.

A victim's mental health, sense of self, and spiritual well-being may be devastated for many years. When a priest sexualizes a relationship with a young person, he robs that young person of the spiritual care the Church should provide. He violates a fundamental religious principle: to protect the vulnerable and to heal the broken. Many victims feel as if their souls have been stolen. They often lose trust in all clergy.

Any abuse that happens in a religious or faith-based community might have the enduring and shattering effects mentioned earlier. Therefore, any church or faith-based community with an abuser, whether that person is a priest, affiliated teacher, youth worker, volunteer, or minister, often carries the same respect and responsibility as a member of the clergy.

Nothing is more tragic than a clergy person who abuses his sacred role; nothing is more traumatic to a congregation than the violation of the basic principles of its faith. What hurts the victim most is not only the cruelty of the offender but also the silence and inaction of bystanders. The community must respond.

Chapter 3

Surviving Sexual Abuse

One Survivor's Story

I learned at an early age that I did not deserve acceptance merely for who I was and that I should never expect it. Perhaps I had myself convinced for too many years that I didn't need anyone and that I had no value. Mostly, though, I was taught that love is taken and not given.

I was extremely shy as a kid. It was my way of not telling. No one thought of my quietness as withdrawal. How I wish someone had. I was a good student as well. I wanted to be good at something. I thought that if I just did something well or right it would make him feel differently about me—my good deeds would make him happy. But they never did. My life became like a game. Pleasing was my goal. I never managed to achieve it with him. I don't know that I really ever could.

I can't tell you the exact date that he first found me alone. That time he didn't stay long. His visits became frequent. I remember what the room looked like, the color of the walls, the shape of the dresser, the shoes on the closet floor, the texture of the bedspread, and the smell of the sheets. I remember the sensation of coming out of my own body so that I wouldn't have to feel anything. And so after a while I became numb. Numb to the literal pain of what he did to me each time—numb to the emotional pain of having these things done to me by my own father.

Each time the abuse took place, my father told me things that fed my self-blame. He told me that what he did was somehow because of me. "I'm doing this because you make me want to do it." In other words, "I can't control myself, and it's your fault." Of course I wanted to be noticed; I wanted to know someone cared about me and for me. What I wanted is every child's birthright: to be adored by somebody and to be loved for who I was, not for my sexual usefulness.

My father began abusing me before I was old enough to understand what was happening to me, even before I had the words to define the experience. It was hard for me to know the difference between what I wanted and what I didn't want because of the insidious way he was able to sneak the abuse upon me. He initiated the abuse slowly, with seemingly innocent stroking and caressing. By the time I was sure I had something to complain about, it was too late. In a little girl, hope struggled to survive. "Maybe this time he will just hug me without touching me there." "Maybe this time he will just listen to me, care for me, and just be my daddy!"

I was robbed of my childhood, my innocence, my ownership of my body, and my sexuality. I withered away. Not all at once, but in one way or another, piece by piece, and finally my whole person, my body, and my soul were taken from me.

All children should be able to expect to be loved. Period. They are entitled to be loved without having *everything* taken from them—without having *anything* taken from them. All children should experience having their needs met without any tradeoffs or paybacks. I experienced none of the love, caring, and trust that belong, unquestioningly, to every child.

I felt guilty and blamed myself for what was happening. Although I wanted someone to know, I was often fearful that someone would indeed find out. What if they did listen? They would think that I had done something wrong. I had no doubt that I would be blamed. Plus I had no assurance that any action would be taken. After all, I saw my power as minimalistic (if at all existent), and whom was I to trust? I ate when the adults in my life told me it was mealtime, and I went to bed when they thought it was best. Adults told me when I had to go to school and to the dentist. I did as I was told.

Consequently I remained quiet and did what my father wanted. I kept the terrible secret to protect him, my family, and myself. If I told anyone what was going on, I believed I would lose everything I loved. It became clear that I had to protect the secret with all my might, not only then but for many years to follow.

Incest is more than rape of the body. It is rape of trust as well. In fact, the sexual aspect of incest is secondary. Someone I trusted, my father, took what he wanted from me, terrorized me, hurt me, humiliated me, controlled me, disgraced me, and shattered the separateness of me. My "no" had no power; my "yes" had no meaning. I learned quickly that even my childlike efforts to understand and have some control over my own life did not matter at all.

Church was my saving grace in high school. I don't really remember how or why I started going, but, nonetheless, I did. Church became a safe haven for me. I loved being there. I felt secure, wanted, respected, and needed—feelings I never experienced at home. I had opportunities to be away from home that provided me with some relief. It would be a long time, however, before I ever really believed that God would or could love someone like me—someone so full of shame.

During my early adult years, I did many things to try to feel worthy. I made a lot of mistakes in hopes of pleasing others. I failed miserably at my work. I found myself in abusive and destructive relationships over and over again. I needed to be needed, but I didn't know how to get my needs met in healthy ways. I didn't know what healthy was.

Many of the memories of what happened were not with me when I left home. As with many incest survivors, I had blocked out most of my childhood memories. But the memories did eventually surface, in the form of nightmares that began to wake me regularly. The nightmares occurred in such a deep state of sleep that I would thrash and wake up screaming, drenched in sweat, sometimes paralyzed. The memories began to pour out, and they eventually consumed me, both night and day. When the memories first began to surface, I would shake my head as if trying to shake off my awareness, as if I were saying: "No! This can't be!" But it was getting harder not to believe what I was experiencing.

When I attended my first therapy group, I knew undeniably that this was where I belonged. Someone there said that she'd "always felt crazy." Hearing that phrase awoke something inside of me. "That's it," I thought. "That's what the feeling is." I too had always felt crazy. And I never told anyone because I was afraid that if I admitted it, somehow that would make it true.

Later, some months into therapy, I was able to analyze my experiences this way: If I, as a child, claim that something awful has happened to me, that someone has done something terrible to me, and if everyone around me acts as if nothing is the matter . . . then either I must be crazy, or everyone around me is crazy. When you are a kid and your life depends on all these important people, you have no choice: of course I must be the crazy one. I felt crazy to be upset when "nothing has been done to me," crazy to feel so uncomfortable around someone who "loves me so much" and "would never do things like that," crazy to see and feel things that "aren't happening" according to everyone around me, and crazy to be so unhappy about what my father did to me, for, after all, he said it was "love." And of course I needed to believe that he really did love me. As long as I needed to preserve that image of him as a loving father, I was willing to lie to myself.

Shame . . . it is a deep sense of worthlessness, a sense of innate badness, not in relation to one's action but to one's very self. As a child victim of incest, I felt shame as well as guilt. Guilt says, "I did something wrong." But shame says, "I am bad because of what I am doing."
I was good at shame. In the beginning I blamed myself a lot. I felt soiled and spoiled, contaminated by the dirty acts that I "permitted" or "even asked for."

I came to learn that the abuse had nothing to do with me. My father chose me because he could have this sexual power over me, not because of something I did or said. I had to let go of the distorted sense of power I thought I had and realize that I was simply invisible to him. Letting go of my own beliefs was difficult because it was easier for me to feel that I was bad than to believe that I was of no importance. This realization was worse than being invisible; it was being nothing. Not being.

My father's anger and his abuse of me were terrifying for a young girl to deal with. I was a smart girl, and I knew I couldn't go anywhere. I needed my parents to take care of me, so I made up a father! I forgot about the clenched fist. I forgot about the sexual molestation. I didn't remember the years he did not talk to me.

Now when I think back on my life with my father, I feel sadness. I loved him so very much, and he shattered that love. His irresponsible actions ruined our relationship forever. He damaged my ability to trust myself. With time and counseling, the fear passed and I came to know how good it felt to no longer carry the secret and that I was no longer the receptacle of my father's disease.

Rather than developing an awareness of myself, I was taught to deny myself. I knew that in life I was expected to accommodate the needs of others, and I often expected to be hurt in doing so. I valued being needed because I could not imagine being wanted.

Fear of abandonment has permeated my adult life. I was terrified of losing what little I was getting from the relationships in which I was involved. Deprivation had made me desperate. I could not see during all that time how little my relationships were offering me. To let go and rely on myself was not a choice; there was no self on which to rely. Hungrily I went from one relationship to another. I let other people choose me, rather than selecting whom I wanted in my life. I had no framework for trust. When I began therapy, I did not understand what trust meant or how trust develops between people. Trust is a feeling of safety, comfort, and security with a person. I was incapable of trusting. I had learned that words don't mean what they say, that things are not always what they seem, and that what appears safe is generally not to be believed. I did not dare being vulnerable because my experience had taught me that vulnerability resulted in being taken advantage of. How could I trust anyone ever again?

My greatest struggles have been in validating my feelings. It is hard for me to feel entitled to complain about what happened to me. Finally, in the safety of a group, in a therapist's office, and in the arms of a friend, I find my pain. There is so much pain. Every time I tell about it, I hurt in a new place. Often I want it to just be over. I want to be rid of it. But in my pain lie the wisdom and understanding that will help me grow as a valuable human being. Now, instead of trying not to cry and trying to "figure it out," I am learning to let myself sit with the hurt and fully experience my feelings, for the pain will show me, teach me how to live. The pain is not entirely all mine. It is the pain of the little girl I was long ago. Think of a kid. Think of a kid with sad eyes. She cries for help for the child inside. I am now moving beyond surviving to work for the quality of life that I deserve. I have unlocked and broken the secret, taken my power back, shed the guilt and self-blame of the experience, and learned, finally, to be angry with what was done to me instead of blaming myself. I refuse to live my life consumed in hatred. Forgiveness has been offered; reconciliation has yet to come.

Rebuilding self-esteem is complicated and difficult. I have struggled from seeing myself as bad to seeing myself as weak. Learning to accept that I am not to blame was a major victory; learning to stop calling myself a victim and start calling myself a survivor is another. To finally define myself not by my past but by my potential, not through what was done to me but through what I am making of myself, is the ultimate step to reclaiming my life and myself.

This story of mine is no longer about crucifixion and death. It is now a story about ascension and resurrection. This journey of recovery has been slow, tortuous, exhilarating, overwhelming, frightening, empowering, devastating, and freeing. It has been a journey that is now bringing me great blessings and joy. And it is my journey to travel. And finally I know that I no longer travel alone.

Part B

Training, Education, and Listening Sessions

Session 1

A Session for Ministry Leaders and Volunteers

Session Overview

Ideally all those involved in ministry with young people have clear and pure intentions in their work with adolescents. Although admirable, good intentions are simply not enough. Many well-meaning adults must learn appropriate ways to minister to and with young people. This session is intended for any adults, including young adults, who are involved in youth ministry efforts at a school or church. These people might include volunteers, catechists, aides, and advocates who work with teens for one time only, who are involved regularly, or who have been around for years. The session provides the participants with an overview of healthy adolescent development and offers information on how to recognize sexual abuse indicators.

Outcomes

- The learner will recognize various signs of abuse and potential risk for abuse.

- The learner will identify tools that will build awareness and encourage proactive responses to potentially abusive relationships within the parish or school community.
- The learner will be empowered to implement resources that will contribute to creating and maintaining a safe and sacred community.

Facilitation

The facilitator's role is to allow for an open discussion where all participants share (if they choose to do so). The facilitator should introduce the purpose of the session and the guidelines for the discussion. It is essential that the facilitator of this session have excellent listening skills. The facilitator should not be a member of the clergy. The presence of or cofacilitation by a professional psychologist or social worker is strongly suggested. At a minimum, a professional should be readily accessible if needed.

Session at a Glance

- Quiz Time (25 minutes)
- Signs and Signals (15 minutes)
- Listening Well (15 minutes)
- Prayer: Each Is Valuable (10 minutes)

Session Content

Quiz Time (25 minutes)

Preparation

Gather the following items:

- ☐ pens or pencils, one for each participant
- ☐ newsprint and markers
- ☐ copies of handout 1, "Quiz Time," one for each participant

1. Welcome the participants and provide a brief overview of the session. Then distribute to each participant a copy of handout 1 and a pen or pencil. Invite them to take a few minutes to complete the handout on their own. Allow about 5 to 7 minutes for them to do this.

2. When everyone has completed the quiz, review each question and provide the participants with the correct answers and additional information as noted below:

- Can a person be sexually abused without being touched?
  - **Answer.** Yes. In reality, sexual abuse can take on various forms. It can be actions involving sexual intercourse to fondling under or over the clothes to the sexual exploitation of children where no direct physical action is perpetrated but where they are in the presence of someone who is clearly becoming sexually aroused by their presence. For example, a perpetrator might expose a child to pornography while watching to see what the child does in response to this exploitation, or a perpetrator might take photos of a naked child for personal sexual stimulation.
- What percentage of the time does a victim of sexual abuse know his or her abuser?
  - **Answer.** 90 percent. Sexual abuse happens most often with people who know the victim. Stranger abuse is fairly rare. Abuse also happens in familiar places. Abusers are most often fathers, stepfathers, siblings, aunts, uncles, baby-sitters, caretakers, or supervisors. Normally the victim of sexual abuse knows his or her abuser.
- Who is the most common sex offender?
  - **Answer.** A white married male. Perpetrators of sexual abuse usually know their victims. Most often, sex offenders are white married males, but sex offenders can be found in every socioeconomic classification, every race, every sexual orientation, and every description. Contrary to the impression given by the media, sexual offenders are also found in every religious background.
- What is a person called who is attracted sexually to a child between the ages of fourteen and eighteen?
  - **Answer.** An ephebophile. An ephebophile is an individual who is attracted sexually to a pubertal child or adolescent in the age range of fourteen to eighteen. Ephebophiles tend to have significantly fewer victims and seem less fixated than pedophiles.
- What is the percentage of priests in the United States who are reported sex offenders?
  - **Answer.** 0.2 percent to 4 percent in the low range; 4 percent to 8 percent in the high range. The Center for Applied Research in the Apostolate at Georgetown University estimates the total number of priests in the United States to be about 47,000. It estimates that 79 percent of these priests are diocesan, with the remaining 21 percent being religious order priests. Some estimate that 0.2 percent to 4 percent, or minimally between 100 and 2,000 priests, are sex offenders.
- Under Church law can a priest choose or be forced to resign from being a priest as a result of his sexual offenses?

    - **Answer.** No. Theology surrounding the priesthood changed after the Council of Trent in the sixteenth century. The priest's very being was defined as forever changed as a result of simply being ordained into the "order" of "priest." In this Catholic framework, ordination to the priesthood is such a significant and altering event that even if a priest decides to renounce his duties, he can never technically resign from being a priest. "He cannot become a layman again in the strict sense, because the character imprinted by ordination is forever"[5] (*CCC*, no. 1583). In being ordained, the priest, as stated in Hebrews 5:6, is considered "a priest forever, according to the order of Melchizedek."
- Do most children readily tell an adult, usually a parent, when something serious like sexual abuse happens to them?
    - **Answer.** No. Children frequently do not tell about being sexually abused, especially if the abuser is a member of the family. Those who have broken their silence are very often not believed as children or as adults. Abused children often struggle with the thought that they must be very bad for God to allow the abuse to happen in the first place.
- Why is abuse not often reported immediately?
    - **Answer.** There are often no witnesses. The key to understanding why sexual abuse is not reported immediately is recognizing that so often the abuse happens in a secluded place. The abuser most often is someone who has power and influence over the child and who has used that power and influence to both groom and silence the child. Victims often want to tell and want to have the abuse stopped. As children, victims do not possess the mental capacity to break away from the power of their abuser to report what is happening.
- Are most offenders prosecuted and punished?
    - **Answer.** No. Only a few of those who commit sexual assaults are apprehended and convicted for their crimes. Most convicted sex offenders are eventually released into the community under probation or parole supervision.
- Of those who abuse, how many were abused themselves?
    - **Answer.** 30 percent. Most sex offenders were not sexually assaulted as children, and most children who are sexually assaulted do not sexually assault others. Not all abusers are acting out of revenge for their past victimization. Adolescent sex offenders do not always become adult offenders. Factors that may influence a victim to become an abuser include when the abuse happened, what kind of treatment the victim received, how the family reacted to the abuse, how many times the abuse took place, and what kind of abuse was inflicted on the victim.

3. Ask the participants the following questions:

- What surprised you in this exercise?
- Is there anything in the quiz that is not surprising to you or that you already knew?
- How realistic do you think these facts are?

Variation

Create an informational and interactive bulletin board in a visible location, using the questions from the quiz. Create flip cards or tabs so that readers can take the quiz while reading the information on the bulletin board.

Signs and Signals (15 minutes)

1. Ask the participants to think back to when they were teenagers and consider their answers to the following questions. Allow them to think about the answers privately without saying them out loud to the group. Pause for a moment between each question to allow for personal reflection.

- Who from your teen years was a significant and supportive adult?
- What made that person significant and supportive?
- What were some of the issues that you or your peers struggled with?

2. Invite a few of the participants to share their responses, or if time permits, divide the large group into small groups of four and invite them to share their responses with one another.

3. Share with the participants the following information:

- People must understand and appreciate normal adolescent development before looking at what might be abnormal reactions to experiences and sexual abuse.
- Odd and seemingly weird developments in a once "happy and normal" person occur inside a teenager.
- For young people, changes in liking and disliking what the body feels and looks like often are accompanied by sudden and dramatic mood fluctuations that seem not to have much foundation in everyday events and perceptions.
- Young people are often at odds with authority in some way because they see a substantial need to reconfigure their world and the meanings within their world.
- Risk-taking behavior is often characteristic of this age not only because of age-appropriate questioning but also because teens and preteens don't have the developmental capacities to predict long-term effects. Testing limits is a way for them to test whom they can

trust. As a result, they often come up against self-doubts, valid fears, persistent conflicts, and ruminative preoccupations.

- If young people have been given inaccurate or no information about sex, that information becomes the foundation upon which their adaptive or developmentally appropriate curiosity is based. If a child has gone through previous developmental phases well, with proper environmental and familial supports and adequate coping skills, she or he will have the best chance to progress—as best as can be expected—through this developmental stage called adolescence.

4. Invite the participants to take a moment to reflect on the following question:

- From where or whom did you learn about sex and sexuality?

Again, invite a few participants to share their responses with the large group, or divide the large group into smaller groups for sharing.

5. Present the following information:

- Fear, a sense of betrayal, helplessness, a feeling of entrapment, and a feeling of not wanting to cause trouble are all reasons why most victims remain silent.
- Most often, victims will tell of the abuse years later, if at all, because they feel too ashamed, too guilty, and somewhat responsible for the offense.
- Victims often report accidentally or purposefully because they are feeling anger (primary reason), because they want to protect other siblings from abuse, because the abuse is so painful and intolerable, because they have medical needs (an STD or a pregnancy), because the perpetrator is absent, or because a safe relationship has entered their life.
- Victims often have excessive fear and physical reactions and behavioral and emotional changes (beyond those mentioned above).
  - **Fear reactions.** Excessive fear reactions include fear of previously liked places and people; fear of particular situations, like being alone or being in the dark; troubled sleeping, accompanied by nightmares or sleep disturbances; startled responses to loud noises or voices; and possible paranoia about being watched or chased.
  - **Physical reactions.** Physical reactions to abuse can include more frequent headaches, stomachaches, or body aches; feeling overly tired or unmotivated; heart palpitations; troubled breathing; and various sexual reactions, including being overly fearful of contact to being promiscuous.
  - **Behavioral and emotional changes.** These kinds of changes might include aggressiveness (verbal or physical), defiance, sexu-

alized behavior, poor hygiene, excessive drug or alcohol use, depression, withdrawal, isolation, changes in eating habits, changes in academic performance, self-mutilation, suicide attempts, delinquent behavior, and excessive risk-taking behaviors.

Listening Well (15 minutes)

Preparation

Using two sheets of newsprint, create two separate outlines of a young person. For visual effect make the outlines life-size (if space permits). Post the outlines on the wall.

1. Present the following information to the group, using these or similar words:

- Sexual abuse is often not reported immediately because the abuse usually happens in a secluded place where there are no witnesses.
- A sexual offender usually is someone who has power and influence over a child and who has used that power and influence to both groom and silence the child.
- The importance of understanding these essential aspects cannot be understated.
- How then do we find out about abuse?
- Most often victims will tell of their abuse years later, if at all, because they felt too ashamed, too guilty, and somehow responsible for the offense.
- This tells us that, as leaders in ministry, we need to be extraordinarily aware of the young people in our community and how they relate and respond to one another and to adults. The best key is prevention because detection might prove to be very difficult.
- We should all be aware of and looking out for significant changes and behavior that are out of the ordinary.
- Knowing that abuse is so often covered up and kept secret by both the abuser and the victim, ministry leaders must make an effort to be aware, educated, and consistently acting as advocates for young people by being present, supportive, and participative in youth programs and activities.

2. Refer to the two outlines of young people that you made before the session. Tell participants that they will be creating two young "paper people." One young person will be filled with unhealthy characteristics, the other with healthy characteristics. Tell the participants that they are to decipher which characteristics contribute to making up a happy and healthy individual and which ones do not. If you think the group can generate its own list of characteristics, allow them to do so.

If not, use the list below to get started and ask the group to add any of their own. Use markers to write words and phrases directly on each "paper person." Note: The examples do not necessarily point specifically to sexual or any other kind of abuse.

- adult mentors
- sad
- feeling hopeless
- no follow-through
- eating well
- going to school
- involved in a school activity
- teen pregnancy
- service in the community
- participates in church services or religious programs
- wants to help others
- being abused
- confused
- easily distracted
- angry
- wants to do well
- lies
- has goals
- dreams about the future
- listens to others
- teases others
- socially withdrawn
- seeks advice
- self-confident
- sexually active
- not motivated
- does not value friendship

3. The two paper people that the group has created may seem to be extreme—one is a super human, and one is negatively extreme. Ask the participants to respond to the following questions in the large group:

- Does either of these paper people realistically represent teenagers today?
- What changes would you make to create a sample of a realistic teenager today?

4. One at a time, choose a sampling of words taken from each extreme paper person and then ask the group the following questions:

- What kind of responses do we have when someone is __________?
- What kind of responses would motivate a teenager to seek a healthier lifestyle and to address issues that may be damaging?
- As adult leaders in the community, how can we best prepare ourselves to assess the healthy and unhealthy behaviors of the youth in our community?

5. Stress to the participants the following points:

- This activity points to several, but certainly not all, issues that surround the lives of adolescents today. When adults care about the welfare of the young people in their community, addressing unhealthy issues and supporting healthy issues will do the following:
  - set a precedent for healthy behavior
  - provide tools for young people to gain insight and knowledge on how to grow into a healthy adult
  - increase the chance that other adults will take initiative to respect and support the young people in the community

6. Ask the participants to respond out loud to the following questions. If the group is large, invite the participants to share their responses with one other person.

- What do you wish you had heard as a teenager about teen issues?
- What do you feel that we, as a group of adult leaders, can do, say, or be to improve the way we support young people in their spiritual development and self-esteem?

Prayer: Each Is Valuable (10 minutes)

Preparation

Gather the following items:

- ☐ a Bible
- ☐ a table to hold the Bible and the name cards (in a basket or pile)
- ☐ pins, tape, or tools to attach name cards
- ☐ pens or pencils, one for each participant
- ☐ a standing board (cardboard or other) that can be hung or placed in a visible area
- ☐ a list of the first names of the young people in your school, program, or parish (active or inactive)
- ☐ a copy of resource 1, "Name Cards," enough so that there is one name card for every teen in your school, parish, or program

Cut out each name card and have the cards ready to use for the prayer. For a different effect, cut pieces of ribbon, one for each young person on the list. If the number of names significantly outweighs the number of adults who will be at the session, you may want to prepare the cards or ribbons with names on them prior to the beginning of the prayer. Another option would be to use different colors of paper or ribbon to signify different ages or genders or other statistics that might be significant and helpful for Church leaders to know.

Before the session starts, ask for a volunteer to proclaim the Scripture reading when you are ready for it.

1. Share the following points with the participants:

- Throughout the time that we are learning about abuse, we must stay focused on prayer and placing our needs and the needs of the community in God's hands.
- In this prayer we will have the opportunity to see how many young people are affected by our efforts and how many are counting on the healthy choices of the adults in their community to keep them safe.

2. Divide the list of names among the participants and ask each person to come to the table and write each name on a separate card. They can leave their cards at the table when they are finished. This will take some time. Give the process the time that it needs. The time it takes will be a direct link to the effort and time it will take to work toward reaching all the young people in the faith community.

3. When all names have been written on a card, share the following points with the participants:

- Our God knows each of us intimately, completely, and lovingly.
- As you listen to the following psalm, consider both how much God loves you and cherishes you and how much the young people of our community seek to know that they are loved and cherished by God.

4. Invite the volunteer to come forward to proclaim Psalm 139 in its entirety. While the psalm is being read, have all other participants come forward in silence and one at a time take name cards from the piles and attach them to the standing board until all the names are on the board.

5. Conclude with a prayer similar to this:

Loving and guiding God, you know our every thought, our every desire, our every hope. We gather to name the youth who live, play, study, work, dream, hope, and believe among us. Help us to cherish all young people as you do. Work through each of us to bring all children the security and safety they so deserve and need. Empower us with your strength and wisdom to work together to create a safe place for our community's young people so that they may continue to love and serve you and one another. We offer these young people and their needs in your name: *[If time permits, say aloud each name that is posted on the standing board.]* Using these name cards as our reminder of the young people who seek our leadership, we ask you to help us to trust in your guidance. We ask all this through Jesus Christ, our Lord. Amen.

6. At the conclusion of the session, place the standing board in a visible place, such as the staff or faculty lounge, front desk, leader's meeting room, or chapel.

Variation

Copy the above prayer onto small cards. Use these prayer cards in place of the name cards. At the conclusion of the prayer, ask each adult to take a prayer card with a young person's name. If there are more adults than prayer cards, post the cards in a visible location in your community with an invitation that other community members take a prayer card to pray specifically for that teen.

Quiz Time

1. Can a person be sexually abused without being touched?
   a. Yes **b.** No

2. What percentage of the time does a victim of sexual abuse know his or her abuser?
   a. 50 percent **b.** 66 percent **c.** 75percent **d.** 90 percent

3. Who is the most common sex offender?
   a. a homosexual
   b. a poor person
   c. a white married male
   d. someone who was previously abused

4. What is a person called who is attracted sexually to a child between the ages of fourteen and eighteen?
   a. pedimanic **b.** ephebophile **c.** araphilic **d.** pedophile

5. What is the lowest percentage of priests in the United States who are reported sex offenders?
   a. 0.2 percent to 4 percent **b.** 3 percent **c.** 4 percent to 5 percent **d.** 8.5 percent

6. Under Church law, can a priest choose or be forced to resign from being a priest as a result of his sexual offenses?
   a. Yes **b.** No

7. Do most children readily tell an adult, usually a parent, when something serious like sexual abuse happens to them?
   a. Yes **b.** No

8. Why is abuse not often reported immediately?
   a. there are often no witnesses
   b. children are good storytellers and do not always know what they are saying
   c. most reported cases turn out to be false accusations
   d. victims do not want to tell anyone

9. Are most offenders prosecuted and punished?
   a. Yes **b.** No

10. Of those who abuse, how many were abused themselves?
    a. 10 percent **b.** 22 percent **c.** 30 percent **d.** 48 percent

Name Cards

We trust into your hands: ______________.	We trust into your hands: ______________.	We trust into your hands: ______________.
We trust into your hands: ______________.	We trust into your hands: ______________.	We trust into your hands: ______________.
We trust into your hands: ______________.	We trust into your hands: ______________.	We trust into your hands: ______________.

Resource 1: Permission to reproduce this resource for program use is granted.

A Session for Ministry Leaders and Volunteers

Session Overview

Even a well-planned program can be subject to risk. Often seemingly harmless activities are overlooked as potentially dangerous situations. An effective ministry leader must look at each aspect of a program with a critical eye to ensure the well-being of the young people. The following session promotes critical thinking and invites catechists, facilitators, and ministry volunteers into a comfortable understanding of the significant role of a leader.

Outcomes

- The learner will create a system of resources for reaching out to young people in crisis.
- The learner will understand the difference between appropriate and inappropriate relationships with young people.
- The learner will identify his or her role in the community as a key leader in preventing child sexual abuse.

Facilitation

The facilitator's role is to allow for an open discussion where all the participants share (if they choose to do so). The facilitator should introduce the purpose of the session and the guidelines for the discussion. It is essential that the facilitator of this session have excellent listening skills. The facilitator should not be a member of the clergy. The presence of or cofacilitation by a professional psychologist or social worker is strongly suggested. At a minimum, a professional should be readily accessible if needed.

Session at a Glance

- What If? (30 minutes)
- Community Search (20 minutes)
- Self-Search (25 minutes)
- Prepared and Empowered (5 minutes)

Session Content

Preparation

Gather the following items:

- ☐ newsprint and markers
- ☐ pens or pencils, one for each participant
- ☐ copies of handout 2, "Agency Information Card," one for each small group of five
- ☐ copies of handout 3, "Reflective Journaling," one for each participant
- ☐ a Bible
- ☐ board of names created in session 1

- Photocopy and cut apart resource 2, "Ministry Scenarios," so that each small group has one scenario.
- Post the following discussion questions on newsprint:
  - What is happening in the scenario?
  - Who is involved, and what is the activity?
  - What benefits does an activity like this have in a ministry program?
  - What are the areas of risk involved in an activity like this?
  - What are the possible outcomes of this activity? Consider both positive and negative outcomes.
  - As ministry leaders, what steps should we take to ensure that this activity will help create a safe and sacred environment for the young people?

- Gather newspaper articles, Web site printouts, and pamphlets from various local and national agencies that advocate child abuse prevention and provide crisis assistance. Choose agencies such as family and teen counseling services, rape crisis centers, child protective services, foster care programs, diocesan child protection services, foundations for prevention and assistance, domestic shelters, and preventative programs and services. You may also wish to review and makes copies of the materials found in Part A of this manual. Refer to Part C for a listing of resources, organizations, and Web sites that contain additional information. Familiarize yourself with the information prior to the session so that you can answer clarifying questions as needed.
- Make arrangements to meet in a space that allows for the participants to separate for individual reflection. The chapel, church, a space outside, or a space in or near the large-group meeting room will work.
- Display the standing board of names created in session 1.
- Ask a volunteer to be prepared to proclaim Romans 5:5 as a closing to the prayer.

What If? (30 minutes)

1. Welcome the participants and provide a brief overview of the session as follows:

- We are going to take a look at some average activities that young people might participate in within the faith community.
- Although each activity may be worthwhile to the young people, each activity can also hold risks if we as leaders do not plan thoroughly.
- I will divide the large group into small groups, and I will give each small group one situation, or scenario. Your task will be to evaluate the possible risks involved.
- Each group's goal is to review the given scenario with a critical eye and to anticipate what could be modified or changed to avoid unnecessary and risky situations.

2. Divide the large group into groups of five or six. Give a copy of one scenario from resource 2 to each small group. If there are more groups than scenarios, you will want to hand out duplicate scenarios or create some that are specific to your community. Having groups duplicate scenarios may offer a variety of insight to the same situation.

3. Ask one person in each small group to read aloud the group's scenario. Then refer the participants to the discussion questions you have posted on newsprint. Instruct the groups to spend some time responding to the questions. Allow ample time for thorough discussion in the groups.

4. Invite each small group to plan a presentation of their discussion through role-playing. Provide the participants with the following instructions:

- Each role-play should be presented in two parts.
- In part one, the group role-plays only what is written on the scenario card.
- In part two, the group plays out possible outcomes of the situation. You will want to role-play as many outcomes as possible.
- Remember, the idea is to encourage thinking about all the possible outcomes. The ideal or preferred outcome should be a sincere option that takes into consideration the mission of creating a safe environment for young people.
- Be as creative as you wish.
- You have several minutes to plan for and develop your role-plays.

5. Invite each small group to come forward and present their role-plays. In each presentation the group presenting should say which of the possible outcomes created would be the most ideal situation and what steps they might take in a real youth activity to create the best possible scenario. Add appropriate comments and make appropriate suggestions and adjustments to their commentary as needed.

Community Search (20 minutes)

1. Share the following points with the participants:

- As leaders in ministry, it is our responsibility to prevent abuse whenever possible.
- It is also the obligation of a leader in the community to provide resources for young people or families in need when abuse occurs.
- Ministry leaders are not licensed counselors or caseworkers. None of us should ever assume the role of a psychological professional in times of crisis.
- Service agencies do exist in our local communities, and we all need to be aware of where to help a family turn for assistance in times of need.
- This activity will help the group learn about child abuse services that are available in the local community.

2. Divide the large group into small groups of five to six people. You may want to change the groups from the previous activity so that the participants will have a chance to meet and work with a variety of people throughout the session.

3. Using the information gathered before the session, assign one agency to each small group. You will also need to provide each group with a pen or pencil and a copy of handout 2. Instruct each small group to familiarize themselves with the agency information and then to complete the handout using that information. Allow the groups 10 minutes to complete the card.

4. When all the groups have completed the assigned task, ask for a representative from each small group to present the information form to the large group. Add information or make comments where necessary.

Variation

Consider arranging for a panel presentation of representatives from local agencies to speak to the group, or arrange for a tour of a local agency to learn about its services and facilities. After the session you could also include information from the cards in a youth ministry, parish, or school newsletter, bulletin, or Web site. You could also post the information on a bulletin board or area accessible to teens and their families, along with other information, such as facts about sexual abuse.

Self Search (25 minutes)

1. Share the following points with the participants:

- The role of leaders in a ministry program is crucial. The continued support of adults from the community provides young people and their parents with the reassurance that all opportunities for spiritual, social, and emotional growth among adolescents will be safe.
- Adults must be present when young people gather in the community. The absence of adult involvement in youth programming can be damaging. Youth will not know the support of the adult community unless that support is seen, heard, voiced, and repeated.
- Young people need the healthy involvement of adults to both encourage them and challenge them in their spiritual growth.

2. Instruct the participants to take time for themselves in the form of journaling and personal sharing to recall and reflect on what they have gained from this experience of learning about creating safe and sacred places and how they feel they fit into that creation. Remind them that each adult in the community offers a unique aspect of support to young people and that through personal and serious reflection each is able to recognize, name, and share those unique gifts.

3. Give each participant a copy of handout 3 and a pen or pencil. Invite them to find a space (wherever you have designated for this activity) where they can be alone for 15 minutes. To assist the participants in entering into a time of reflection, guide them through the following centering activity. When guiding the centering activity, be sure to use slow and audible speech. Pause for a calm breath after each sentence.

4. Begin the centering exercise as follows:

Take a deep breath. Loosen and shake your arms and relax them. Wiggle your legs and relax them. Take a deep breath, and then close your eyes. Listen for a moment as we remember back to where we have been. We have taken in a lot of information. We have gained much insight through creative thinking and conversation. And in concern for our children and our Church, we have raised many questions. Our journey is difficult, but it is not impossible. I invite you to welcome in and recognize God's presence among us. Notice the peace that God can offer our hearts. Breathe in the hope that God will fill our minds. Be in God's presence, for God is ever present among us. *[Pause for a moment.]* When you are ready, open your eyes. In silence, pick up your pencil and journaling paper and begin writing. This time is a time for quiet reflection. You will have a chance to share your thoughts when we gather together after 15 minutes.

5. Depending on the needs of the group, invite the participants to gather in pairs or groups of three. Do not allow groups larger than three. Because of the reflective nature of the sharing, larger groups will be time consuming, as the sharing will be specific and individual. Ask the participants to share something about their reflection time with another person. Stress the following points:

- Journaling is a private activity, and no one will be forced to share anything. However, the purpose of the sharing is to gain both support and accountability from fellow leaders in ministry.
- The conversation should be focused on how each person sees herself or himself as a contributor, challenging as it may be, to protecting, helping, and healing young people. Allow the pairs or groups 5 to 10 minutes to share.

Prepared and Empowered (5 minutes)

1. Invite the participants into prayer, using the following or similar words:

- We find many reasons for and symbols of hope in the Scriptures.
- Can anyone name some of them? (Wait for a few responses from the participants. Some possible answers are dove, rainbow, Crucifixion/Resurrection, miracles, Baptism.)

- In addition to the many ways we embrace hope in our lives, the young people we see represented before us are our reason for hoping beyond the difficult and painful issues we have been discussing.
- Their names and faces and mere existence must be the hope that empowers us to continue forward on their behalf. Empowered by our God, who is loving and whose presence is constant, let us offer our prayers of concern and hope.

2. Invite the participants to share out loud the prayers they have written on their journal pages or any spontaneous prayers they have for the continued efforts of protecting the youth of the community. Allow ample time for participants to voice their prayers out loud. Be prepared to begin the prayer yourself if participants are hesitant to speak first.

3. Allow the voices of those gathered to speak as a group prayer, and close with the following Scripture passage: "And hope does not disappoint us, because God's love has been poured into our hearts through the Holy Spirit that has been given to us" (Romans 5:5).

Ministry Scenarios

An overnight lock-in is scheduled for teenagers. A few hours before the event, two adult leaders call to say they won't be able to chaperone. There is not enough time to replace them. Parish and diocesan policy requires a certain adult-to-youth ratio. The ministry leader decides there are enough adults to minimally supervise the evening event.

The pastor of the church enjoys welcoming parishioners as guests into the rectory for dinner and entertaining and does so regularly. He has invited four teenagers from the youth ministry teen leadership team for dinner as a thank-you for their work in the parish community. No other adults will be present.

A married couple is hosting a youth Bible study in their home as they have done for years. They are long-time parishioners and have adolescent children of their own. No other adults are present.

The high school seniors of an all-girls school have been asked by the youth minister to create and host a retreat for the freshman class. A prayer service found in a popular youth ministry manual calls for minimal lighting and teens' placing their hands on one another's shoulders as part of the prayer.

Ministry Scenarios page 2

Teens are involved in a service project at a local agency, painting the exterior of the building. The blazing sun is causing teens to remove outer clothing. The guys are baring their chests, and the women are sporting their sports-bra shirts and rolling up their shorts.

To foster personal relationships in a faith community, the youth minister has made a plan to take a group of teens to lunch each week. Sometimes more than one teen attends lunch with the youth minister, and sometimes, because of last-minute schedule changes, only one teen ends up meeting with the youth minister.

A summer Bible study program hosts about 150 elementary-age children during the summer. About sixty volunteers run the summer program each year. Half of those volunteers are high school teens.

Agency Information Card

What is the name of the agency?

Where is the agency located?

Who founded the agency, and why was it founded? (Is there a mission statement or purpose statement?)

To whom does this agency provide assistance or service?

What services does this agency offer?

How are these services offered? (Are there schedules for sessions or programs? Is there a fee?)

What do you find personally interesting about this agency, and how will knowing about this agency benefit the young people of this community? (More than one group member may provide an answer.)

Reflective Journaling

I got involved in ministry with young people because . . .

Some of the great things I have noticed about the young people in this community are . . .

I wish . . .

I hope . . .

I believe . . .

 Handout 3:

Reflective Journaling page 2

I think that I will be able to help prevent risky situations in our community by (how) . . .

When I think of creating a safe and sacred place for young people, a Scripture passage that comes to mind is . . .

In the next five years in our faith community, I would like to see . . .

My prayer is (write a prayer in your own words) . . .

A Session for Parents and Guardians

Session Overview

Parents play a key role in the success of any ministry program for young people. Parental participation and involvement encourages growth, promotes awareness, and builds trust among the young people and the larger faith community. Parents who are informed and involved in the youth programming will be better able to work as protectors for their own children as well as for all children of the community. Constant communication between parents and ministry leaders can create a greater advocacy network.

Outcomes

- The learner will recognize various signs and indicators of abuse.
- The learner will address fears and stereotypes when facing the topic of child abuse.
- The learner will make a plan for maintaining the community as a safe and sacred place.

Facilitation

The facilitator's role is to allow for an open discussion where all participants share (if they choose to do so). The facilitator should introduce the purpose of the session and any guidelines for the discussion. It is essential that the facilitator of this session have excellent listening skills. The facilitator should not be a member of the clergy. The presence of or cofacilitation by a professional psychologist or social worker is strongly suggested. At a minimum, a professional should be readily accessible if needed.

Session at a Glance

- Facing the Fears (20 minutes)
- Facing the Facts and Figures (25 minutes)
- Facing the Truth (20 minutes)
- Facing Our God (10 minutes)

Session Content

Preparation

Gather the following items:

- ☐ newsprint and markers
- ☐ a copy of handout 1, "Quiz Time," one for each participant
- ☐ a copy of handout 4, "What Every Parent Should Know About Sexual Abuse," one for each participant
- ☐ paper
- ☐ pens or pencils, one for each participant
- ☐ votive candles, one for each participant
- ☐ one large candle
- ☐ a copy of resource 3, "Praying for Our Children," one for each participant

- Place the candles on a prayer table in the center of the meeting space.
- Gather a sampling of facial expressions. Create or draw these expressions, or cut them out of magazines. The expressions should convey a variety of emotions, such as fear, pain, embarrassment, happiness, joy, accomplishment, disappointment, anger, contentment, and surprise. Gather enough facial expressions so that each small group of five to seven participants has access to several different expressions and more than one copy of each.
- Arrange the chairs in groups of five to seven so they are facing one another. The chairs can be around a table or by themselves.

- Write the following discussion questions on a sheet of newsprint and post it on a wall so that all the participants can see it:
  - What emotion does the expression you chose convey?
  - What prompted you to choose this expression?
  - Is your initial reaction to this statement your preferred reaction?
  - How do you wish or hope that you would respond if this situation were real?

Facing the Fears (20 minutes)

1. Welcome the participants and share with them a brief session overview. Then explain that the first activity is an attempt to loosen up their fears a little. The topic of sexual abuse is not an easy one to bring up with children or adults. However uncomfortable the topic might be, it is a necessary one.

2. Divide the large group into groups of no more than eight, and give each small group a variety of the facial expression drawings or cutouts you gathered before the session. Read the following instructions to the participants:

- I will read a series of statements.
- After each statement, quickly choose a facial expression from the pile in the center of your small group and place it in front of your face.
- You will want to make your choice based on your own personal emotional reaction to the situation I present. Do not choose an emotion based on your judgment of the content of the statement. Simply think about how you believe you would feel.

3. Begin by reading the first statement listed below. Be sure to pause after each statement and allow participants to peek at the facial expressions of others in their group so they can see what each person is choosing.

- Your four-year-old asks why he has a penis and his baby sister does not.
- You realize that your preteen daughter will soon have her first period and that you have never talked to her about menstruation.
- Your teenage daughter tells you she wants to know about birth control.
- Your teenage son tells you he wants to know about birth control.
- A teen argues that you shouldn't preach because you had a child before marriage.
- You are watching the news with your seven-year-old child. A story comes on about a recent sexual abuse case involving a local clergy member.

- You just found out that you are required to attend a session at your church about preventing sexual abuse.
- You are watching a movie with your preteen child and are surprised by a sexy bedroom scene.
- Your young daughter is adamantly and unsuccessfully trying to decipher the correct pronunciation of the word *pianist* in a crowded public area.

4. Assign one statement to each small group. Ask each participant to once again lift the facial expression they chose for that statement. Instruct each small group to discuss each member's responses to the questions you have posted on the newsprint.

5. Gather the small groups back into one large group. Ask whether the participants have any insights to share that they have learned from this activity. Allow a few minutes for large-group discussion. Then share the following points with the participants:

- Talking about sex and sexuality, especially in front of teenagers, can be difficult and uncomfortable, but it does not have to be so.
- Our mission in participating in these sessions is not only to educate ourselves on the risk of abuse in our community but also to challenge ourselves and one another to reach beyond what is comfortable for the sake of the safety of our children.
- Throughout the session's discussions, remember that we are gathered together to promote and encourage a safer, and thus more sacred, environment for the young people of our community.

Facing the Facts and Figures (25 minutes)

1. Distribute to each participant a copy of handout 1 and a pen or pencil. Invite them to take a few minutes to answer the questions on the handout on their own. Allow about 5 to 7 minutes for them to do this.

2. When everyone has completed the quiz, review each question and provide the participants with the correct answers and additional information as noted below:

- Can a person be sexually abused without being touched?
  - **Answer.** Yes. In reality, sexual abuse can take on various forms. It can be actions involving sexual intercourse to fondling under or over the clothes to the sexual exploitation of children where no direct physical action is perpetrated but where they are in the presence of someone who is clearly becoming sexually aroused by their presence. For example, a perpetrator might expose a child to

pornography while watching to see what the child does in response to this exploitation, or a perpetrator might take photos of a naked child for personal sexual stimulation.

- What percentage of the time does a victim of sexual abuse know his or her abuser?
  - **Answer.** 90 percent. Sexual abuse happens most often with people who know the victim. Stranger abuse is fairly rare. Abuse also happens in familiar places. Abusers are most often fathers, stepfathers, siblings, aunts, uncles, baby-sitters, caretakers, or supervisors. Normally the victim of sexual abuse knows his or her abuser.
- Who is the most common sex offender?
  - **Answer.** A white married male. Perpetrators of sexual abuse usually know their victims. Most often, sex offenders are white married males, but sex offenders can be found in every socioeconomic classification, every race, every sexual orientation, and every description. Contrary to the impression given by the media, sexual offenders are also found in every religious background.
- What is a person called who is attracted sexually to a child between the ages of fourteen and eighteen?
  - **Answer.** An ephebophile. An ephebophile is an individual who is attracted sexually to a pubertal child or adolescent in the age range of fourteen to eighteen. Ephebophiles tend to have significantly fewer victims and seem less fixated than pedophiles.
- What is the percentage of priests in the United States who are reported sex offenders?
  - **Answer.** 0.2 percent to 4 percent in the low range; 4 percent to 8 percent in the high range. The Center for Applied Research in the Apostolate at Georgetown University estimates the total number of priests in the United States to be about 47,000. It estimates that 79 percent of these priests are diocesan, with the remaining 21 percent being religious order priests. Some estimate that 0.2 percent to 4 percent, or minimally between 100 and 2,000 priests, are sex offenders.
- Under Church law can a priest choose or be forced to resign from being a priest as a result of his sexual offenses?
  - **Answer.** No. Theology surrounding the priesthood changed after the Council of Trent in the sixteenth century. The priest's very being was defined as forever changed as a result of simply being ordained into the "order" of "priest." In this Catholic framework, ordination to the priesthood is such a significant and altering event that even if a priest decides to renounce his duties, he can never technically resign from being a priest. "He cannot become a

layman again in the strict sense, because the character imprinted by ordination is forever"[6] (*CCC*, no. 1583). In being ordained, the priest, as stated in Hebrews 5:6, is considered "a priest forever according to the order of Melchizedek."

- Do most children readily tell an adult, usually a parent, when something serious like sexual abuse happens to them?
  - **Answer.** No. Children frequently do not tell about being sexually abused, especially if the abuser is a member of the family. Those who have broken their silence are very often not believed as children or as adults. Abused children often struggle with the thought that they must be very bad for God to allow the abuse to happen in the first place.
- Why is abuse not often reported immediately?
  - **Answer.** There are often no witnesses. The key to understanding why sexual abuse is not reported immediately is recognizing that so often the abuse happens in a secluded place. The abuser most often is someone who has power and influence over the child and who has used that power and influence to both groom and silence the child. Victims often want to tell and want to have the abuse stopped. As children, victims do not possess the mental capacity to break away from the power of their abuser to report what is happening.
- Are most offenders prosecuted and punished?
  - **Answer.** No. Only a few of those who commit sexual assaults are apprehended and convicted for their crimes. Most convicted sex offenders are eventually released into the community under probation or parole supervision.
- Of those who abuse, how many were abused themselves?
  - **Answer.** 30 percent. Most sex offenders were not sexually assaulted as children, and most children who are sexually assaulted do not sexually assault others. Not all abusers are acting out of revenge for their past victimization. Adolescent sex offenders do not always become adult offenders. Factors that may influence a victim to become an abuser include when the abuse happened, what kind of treatment the victim received, how the family reacted to the abuse, how many times the abuse took place, and what kind of abuse was inflicted on the victim.

3. Ask the participants to discuss the following questions:

- What surprised you in this activity?
- Is there anything in the quiz that is not surprising to you or that you already knew?
- How realistic do you think these facts are?

Variation

Create an informational and interactive bulletin board in a visible location, using the questions from the quiz. Create flip cards or tabs so that readers can take the quiz while reading the information on the bulletin board.

Facing the Truth (20 minutes)

1. Distribute to each participant a copy of handout 4. Share the following points with the participants:

- It is possible that the quiz raised some very real fears, questions, and concerns.
- Some of the information you hear in these sessions will be disturbing and might make you uncomfortable. The information is not meant to create fear or to be offensive.
- Everyone must take responsibility in protecting the children of a faith community.
- Parents have the responsibility and opportunity to be alerted to situations that present possible risks to their children.
- Not all people want to injure children. In fact, the majority of people want to be an asset to the community. It would be ridiculous to assume that every adult has the desire to commit an offense against a child. It would also be naïve to think that no person in the community is capable of committing an offense against a child. Information is meant to help, not to scare.

2. Referring to the handout, review the information provided. Be sure to allow for some discussion or clarifying questions from participants if needed. Then continue with the following comments:

- Awareness regarding the issue of sexual abuse requires an understanding and comprehension of various words, phrases, and definitions. A clearer comprehension of the terminology currently in use provides insight into the issue and can assist adults in recognizing potentially abusive situations. Some primary terms and definitions include:
  - **Child abuse.** Child abuse is any form of intentional or malicious infliction of injury to the detriment of a child's physical, moral, mental, or spiritual well-being.
  - **Sexual misconduct/abuse.** This is any form of sexual conduct that is unlawful; that is contrary to the moral instructions, doctrines, and canon law of the Catholic Church; and that causes injury to another. It may constitute sexual abuse, sexual harassment, or sexual exploitation.

- **Opportunist.** An opportunistic offender seeks out children regularly until caught.
- **Experimenter.** This type of offender abuses as part of sexual exploration.
- **Inadequate and opportunistic.** This type of offender is mentally inadequate or has a stunted mental development.
- **Pedophile.** A pedophile has no sexual interest in adults and is sexually attracted to only prepubescent children, under the age of thirteen.
- **Ephebophile.** An ephebophile is sexually attracted to only post-pubescent children, adolescents between the ages of fourteen and eighteen.
- **Pederast.** This type of offender engages in anal intercourse with boys under the age of eighteen.
- **Nonexclusive.** This type of offender is married or in a relationship with another adult but clearly desires children sexually and uses every opportunity to find situations where sexual contact with a child can happen.
- **Exclusive offender.** This type of offender is attracted only to children.
- **Sex offender.** A sex offender is an individual who is either an ephebophile or a pedophile.

3. Divide the large group into small groups of six. Provide each small group with a sheet of newsprint and a marker. Assign one of the following situations to each group:

- Your young person is leaving the house to attend an athletic event.
- Your young person is going on a date.
- Your young person will be attending a friend's birthday party.
- Your young person will be spending the weekend attending a church-sponsored retreat.
- Your young person has been invited to attend your next-door neighbor's family reunion.
- Your young person's coach offers to transport your child to and from practice.

Should you need additional scenarios, ask for some suggestions from the participants, or add a few based on the types of activities young people are involved with in your community.

4. Offer the following instructions:

- The task for your group is to make a list of questions to ask to be certain that your son or daughter will be as safe as possible in the given situation.

Allow about 5 minutes for the groups to discuss and post their lists on newsprint.

5. Invite each group to present its list. Be sure to incorporate the following points if the participants do not suggest them:

- Always know who is involved in the event—other young people, adults, or people of other age-groups. Is anyone attending whom you or your child would be uncomfortable being around?
- Be clear on the location of the event and how you can access that location if necessary. Do you have an address or a phone number?
- What is the mode of transportation? Be clear on who is driving and whether or not that person is adequately licensed and insured. Find out what general route will be taken. If you are unfamiliar with the driver, will you want to meet him or her beforehand?
- Ask for specifics about the event. When will it begin and end? How can you check in with your child as needed? Whom can you contact to obtain further information?
- Who is in charge of the event or has planned or proposed the event? If the event is a program, is anyone trained or certified for what is happening? What kind of supervision will be provided? Are there any safety issues you should be aware of (e.g., a family party where adults are drinking)?
- When can you expect your child to be home? What are the consequences if she or he is not on time?
- What system do you have in place in case of an emergency? How will you reach your child, or how will your child reach you? Does your child know what steps to take to get to a safe place? Are there other adults your child can turn to in a time of need?
- Completing this activity may seem a bit trivial, but it is a good reminder that you must always be aware of the people our children come in contact with.
- Knowing the answers to these questions is a way of establishing trust between you and your child. Their safety is your primary concern. Gathering this information has nothing to do with being nosy.
- All parents need to make the determination whether they are satisfied with the amount of information their child has given them.
- An effective way to foster this kind of communication is to offer your child information about events in your own life. This does not mean you should share personal details. You are the parent, not the peer. But you can model informative behavior with your child. For example, if you are preparing to go out of town for a work conference, talk about the reason for the conference (educational) and the conference presenters and facilitators (seeking guidance and wisdom from others). Leave information with your family about where you will be staying and your flight arrangements. Make sure they have a way to contact you.

- Letting your loved ones know where you are, what you are doing, and how to find you if you are needed is just good healthy communication.
- Any adult who has contact with young people (school, church, workplace, neighborhood) should make every effort to inform and involve parents about their interactions. Parents deserve to know what is happening with their child when the child is away from home.
- Be sure to offer the same information or considerations to other parents when you are one of the key adults involved in an activity. By initiating such conversations and communication, you can help make safety checks routine for all adults in a community, thus ensuring safer environments for all young people.

6. Provide each participant with a blank sheet of paper and a pen or pencil. Ask each participant to take a moment to think about an upcoming event that will be happening in the life of his or her young person. Some examples could be a school field trip, a church retreat, a parent's travels, a teen's date, a child's weekend soccer game, and so on.

7. Invite the participants to review the lists they generated in step 4 to determine how much they know about the upcoming event or activity. Invite spouses to work together. Ask the parents to think about what further information they would like to know before this event occurs. Allow a few minutes for participants to complete this step.

8. Ask the participants if they have gained any insights from this activity that they would like to share with the group. Add appropriate comments when necessary. Note that this activity can be helpful in alerting the participants to the many factors of busy family life. Assure parents that they can seek the support of other parents in the community. It is likely that the parents gathered will be able to make a commitment to being more informative and communicative with the parents who have gathered for the session. You may even suggest that the participants exchange phone numbers or e-mail addresses to keep in contact to discuss mutual events or activities their children attend.

Facing Our God (10 minutes)

1. Tell the participants that the closing prayer will be an opportunity to pray for their children. Invite them to take a few moments of prayerful silence. Light the large candle you have placed on the prayer table. Then offer the following prayer:

Lord, giver of light, life and hope, you have entrusted your children into our care. We cherish their love and their energy for life. Help us to help them be people of strength, character, and integrity. Share with us the wisdom that will shape their minds. Share with us the love that will guide their hearts. Share with us the courage that will shape their future. Be the light that guides them and us to your glory and goodness.

2. Invite each parent or each set of parents to come forward to the prayer table and light one of the votive candles for their child or children. Ask that they silently offer a prayer for the health and safety of their child or children.

3. When all parents have come forward and all candles are lit, offer the following intercessions. Invite the parents to respond, "Lord, in your mercy, hear our prayer."

- For the courage to see the truth, we pray . . .
- That our actions will be examples for our children, we pray . . .
- For the protection and safety of all children, we pray . . .
- That a loving faith community will nourish our children, we pray . . .
- For the future of the Church and its leaders, we pray . . .
- That we will follow the guiding light of the Gospel of Jesus Christ, we pray . . .

4. To conclude, invite the parents to take a copy of the prayer and a candle home with them to serve as a reminder to pray with and for their children.

What Every Parent Should Know About Sexual Abuse

- All children are vulnerable to sexual abuse regardless of ethnicity, cultural background, or economic background.
- All children have an inherent right to feel loved, valued, and protected.
- Children are best protected when they have the knowledge and skills necessary for their safety and well-being.
- Often there are no physical signs of sexual abuse.
- Many cases of child sexual abuse go unreported because the child is afraid or ashamed to tell anyone what has happened.
- Offenders often threaten to hurt the victim or the victim's family members.
- Many children believe they are to blame for the abuse.
- A victim is never to blame for the abuse. The victim cannot prevent abuse; only the offender can.
- There is little evidence that children make false allegations of abuse; what is more common is a child's denying that abuse happened when it did.

Prayer for Our Children

Lord, giver of light, life, and hope, you have entrusted your children to our care. We cherish their love and their energy for life. Help us to help them be people of strength, character, and integrity. Share with us the wisdom that will shape their minds. Share with us the love that will guide their hearts. Share with us the courage that will shape their future. Be the light that guides them and us to your glory and goodness.

Lord, giver of light, life, and hope, you have entrusted your children to our care. We cherish their love and their energy for life. Help us to help them be people of strength, character, and integrity. Share with us the wisdom that will shape their minds. Share with us the love that will guide their hearts. Share with us the courage that will shape their future. Be the light that guides them and us to your glory and goodness.

Lord, giver of light, life, and hope, you have entrusted your children to our care. We cherish their love and their energy for life. Help us to help them be people of strength, character, and integrity. Share with us the wisdom that will shape their minds. Share with us the love that will guide their hearts. Share with us the courage that will shape their future. Be the light that guides them and us to your glory and goodness.

Lord, giver of light, life, and hope, you have entrusted your children to our care. We cherish their love and their energy for life. Help us to help them be people of strength, character, and integrity. Share with us the wisdom that will shape their minds. Share with us the love that will guide their hearts. Share with us the courage that will shape their future. Be the light that guides them and us to your glory and goodness.

 Resource 3:

A Session for Parents and Guardians

Session Overview

All children deserve to live in a safe and sacred environment. Because parents are the first teachers of their children and know their children best, it is essential to include them in the growing spirituality of their children. Like many members of the Church community, parents seek tools that will empower them to raise children in a safe, loving, and spiritual environment. This session invites parents to seek the support of other parents in the community and to work together with Church leaders and ministers to prevent the various forms of abuse that threaten any community.

Outcomes

- The learner will create a system for responding to young people in a crisis situation.
- The learner will identify his or her key role as a parent in a community of young people.
- The learner will pledge her or his advocacy for young people in the community.

Facilitation

The facilitator's role is to allow for an open discussion where all the participants share (if they so choose). The facilitator should introduce the purpose of the session and any guidelines for the discussion. It is essential that the facilitator of this session have excellent listening skills. The facilitator should not be a member of the clergy. The presence of or cofacilitation by a professional psychologist or social worker is strongly suggested. At a minimum, a professional should be readily accessible if needed.

Session at a Glance

- Beyond Our Control? (25 minutes)
- The Path to Healing and Protection (25 minutes)
- Pledge of Commitment (25 minutes)
- Praying Our Commitment (10 minutes)

Session Content

Preparation

Gather the following items:

- ☐ newsprint and markers
- ☐ masking tape, one roll
- ☐ pens or pencils, one for each participant
- ☐ various magazines for home, beauty, travel, hobbies, teens, and special interests, three to four for each small group of five
- ☐ blank sheets of paper, one for each participant
- ☐ copies of handout 5, "What Is This Ad Selling?" two for each small group
- ☐ copies of handout 6, "Preventing Sexual Abuse," one for each participant
- ☐ a variety of old keys, one for each participant

- Search a popular magazine for two ads that use sex or sexually suggestive language or pictures to sell a product. Display the ads during the session.
- Create a chart on newsprint with the following statements:
  - Be open.
  - Be aware.
  - Persevere.
  - Be realistic.

- Gather examples of pledges, statements, and commitments. Some examples might include the Nicene Creed, a parish mission statement, a company pledge of a product or service, a guarantee or warranty, or the Pledge of Allegiance.
- Attach to each key a ribbon or paper that reads "Safe and Sacred Places."
- On a sheet of newsprint, write "safe & sacred" vertically down the left side.

Beyond Our Control? (25 minutes)

1. Welcome the participants and provide an overview of the session, using the following or similar words:

- Media, in a variety of forms, have a significant amount of time to grab the attention of viewers. Many viewers and consumers are young people.
- We often find mixed messages between what we hear at church and what we hear and see on television, in magazines, and through other advertising venues.
- In this session we will take a closer look at what kinds of messages our young people are receiving.
- This activity is not intended to single out any particular product or advertiser. The purpose is to look at everyday images with a critical eye and to consider the effects of those images on the minds and hearts of young people.
- The focus of this activity is to identify messages in the ads while avoiding conversations about specific products and their value in society.

2. Show the participants the two examples of magazine advertisements you have selected. Invite a few participants to offer their thoughts about the messages the ads convey.

3. Divide the large group into small groups of four or five. Provide each group with three or four magazines, a couple pens or pencils, and two copies of handout 5. Instruct each group to look for advertisements that send mixed messages. Ask each group to locate two specific images and tear them out of the magazine. Each group should also respond to the questions on the handout for each separate ad. Allow several minutes for the groups to accomplish these tasks.

4. Invite each group to post their advertisements and completed handouts on the walls around the room. Then invite all the participants to walk around the room to view the ads and read the comments of each group.

5. Follow the activity with a discussion about the effects of media (magazines, movies, television, and the Internet) on young people, using the following questions with the large group:

- What kinds of media do your children have access to every day?
- How often do you have an opportunity to watch or view these images with your children?
- What did you learn or become aware of as a result of this activity?
- What can a parent do to act as a filter for questionable advertising?

6. Conclude the activity by stating that the elements of media are not beyond our control but that it will take a commitment of time and energy to be aware of what factors outside the home are affecting our children both negatively and positively. These outside messages can critically shape the impressions and decision-making skills of young people.

Variation

This activity can be modified to include television commercials, movies, music, computer games, and Web sites. Gather some video or audio clips to create samples for participants to see and hear. Give the participants a copy of handout 5 to take home to discuss with their children. These handout questions can be used as a guide when discussing issues of media messages at home.

The Path to Healing and Protection (25 minutes)

1. Provide the participants with a copy of handout 6. Review the tips and allow time for discussion or clarifying questions. At the conclusion ask the participants if they have any additional suggestions to add to the list.

2. Divide the large group into small groups of five to seven. Ask the small groups to look at the list on the handout. Tell each participant to choose the items on the list that he or she thinks are the most difficult to achieve. Allow each participant an opportunity to share why she or he believes the item would be difficult. Give the groups enough time so that each person can share at least one point.

3. Ask the small groups to take their conversation one step further. It is not enough to name what we think is difficult or even impossible; we must then challenge ourselves to decide what we want to do about it. For each obstacle or concern that was raised in the first part of the group discussion, the group must determine a change, goal, or option for a solution. Encourage group members to help one another and to rely on the wisdom of the other participants.

4. Gather the participants back into the large group and ask for a sampling of sharing from each group.

5. Refer the participants to the newsprint you have posted, and then make the following comments:

- Talking about the possibility of sexual abuse is not comfortable or pleasant. Expanding our level of comfort with difficult issues will prove highly beneficial to keeping our children safe. **Be open.**
- Continued education about the issues of sexual abuse and a high awareness of what is happening in our own community will contribute to the building of a consistently safe environment for our children. **Be aware.**
- Keep talking and keep listening. Collective and consistent efforts to educate the community will pay off. Because sexual abuse is a difficult reality to face, success will not come with ease. **Persevere.**
- Sessions or programs cannot prevent every possible crisis situation. People have the gift of free will and choice. Just as offenders have the free will to choose poorly, advocates for children have the free will to choose wisely. Sexual abuse may strike our community, but prevention and preparation will make a huge difference. **Be realistic.**

Pledge of Commitment (25 minutes)

1. Provide each participant with a blank sheet of paper and a pen or pencil. Instruct them to work for five minutes creating a pledge to their children. Offer examples of what a pledge signifies by showing the examples you have gathered. Have your examples available for participants to look at and refer to while creating their pledge.

2. Tell the participants that it is not important that their words be eloquent. A parent's own words to his or her children, no matter how simple or fragmented, are meaningful and valuable. Encourage the participants to work on their pledges individually, even though spouses may be attending the session together.

3. Divide the large group into small groups of three or four. Allow the participants 7 to 10 minutes to share something significant from their pledge that they would like to communicate to other parents.

4. Call the participants back to the large group. Ask them to voice out loud some sample phrases from their individual pledges. Combine the phrases to create a group pledge. Be sure to create this combination within the context of the session so that parents feel and know they have the deciding power in what the group pledge will include.

5. Ask whether any participants are willing to make a public statement about their commitment by placing their pledge in a visible area of the community property. The pledges could be posted on a bulletin board or published in the community newsletter, Web site, or bulletin. If you choose to display the pledges in a public place, be sure to return a copy of each pledge to its owner so that all participants can take their pledges home to share with their children. When displaying the group pledge, create a space where other members of the community can read and sign it. Or make copies of the pledge in the parish bulletin or other flyer so that community members can post it in their own homes.

Praying Our Commitment

1. Thank the parents for participating in this important series of sessions. Distribute a key to each participant. Hold a key in your hand and show it to the participants. Share the following points with the participants:

- All of us gathered, and all those in the community who have and will gather to learn about issues of child abuse, hold the keys to unlock the doors of safety, protection, and security to the children of the faith community.
- Ignorance will keep the doors of communication and awareness locked, but with education, concern, and conversation, we hold the keys to doors that need not be locked.

2. Refer to the newsprint with "safe & sacred" written down the left side. With a prayerful tone, invite the participants to add words or phrases they consider keys to unlocking the doors that lead to prevention of abuse and the promotion of their children's safety. Examples might include:

- S – secure environment
- A – advocate for children's needs
- F – focus on the real issues
- E – embrace hope

  &

- S – spirituality is essential
- A – actively participate in the community
- C – Christ-centered life
- R – recognize signs and signals
- E – education
- D – determination

Encourage the participants to be creative. Add your own thoughts only as an example if participants seem unable to come up with words or phrases of their own. If time permits, allow the participants to add more than one word or phrase to each letter.

3. Invite the participants to offer up their prayers of petition for one another and for their children and the community. Close the intercessions with this prayer:

> Loving and knowing God, guide our children safely to your protection. Help us to use the keys that will open the doors to safe and sacred places for all children.

4. Invite the participants to take their keys home and hang them in a visible place where their family can see them often.

What Is This Ad Selling?

What product or service is this ad selling?

What images or words are being used to sell it?

What message or messages is this ad sending that conflict with Christian values?

Believing that this is a worthwhile product, how could you change the ad to benefit both the seller and the values, self-worth, and emotional safety of the buyer, listener, or reader?

 Handout 5:

Preventing Sexual Abuse

- Supervise! Know whom your child is talking to at all times.
- Parental controls—use them and learn about them!
- Tell your child you will monitor his or her relationships. Be sure to follow up with that claim.
- Talk to your child's friends about what is happening online.
- If you don't know about the Internet and cyber sex, become informed.
- Young people need to know that their bodies are sacred. Talk openly about safe versus unsafe touch.
- Create and encourage your child to develop support and trust with significant adults whom they can trust.
- A good rule of thumb: If someone enjoys being around your child more than you do, there is a problem.
- Nothing is more sacred than communication; nothing is more preventive! Research points to this aspect of prevention as being key. Good communication assumes mutual respect regardless of any information a child might share.
- Open discussion about sexual matters, although it may be uncomfortable, needs to be pursued. If not to you, to whom will your child turn?
- Know the adults, peers, and the families of peers with whom your child relates. Ask about all that happened with your child when you were not with her or him. Be curious.
- Your values are key for your child to know; however, your child needs you most of all. As the saying goes, L-O-V-E means or is spelled T-I-M-E.
- Be there and know where your child is and what he or she is doing. Meet all parents who will be supervising your child in whatever capacity. Do not assume anything about anyone.
- Show your child that it is okay to say no when someone she or he knows and cares about does something he or she does not like.
- Set and respect family boundaries.
- Speak up when you see "warning sign" behaviors.
- Practice talking about difficult topics, such as sexual abuse, with other adults.
- Be sure you are comfortable saying the proper names of body parts before you teach them to your child.
- Teach your child that secrets about touching are not okay.
- Set up a family safety plan that is easy to remember.
- List for yourself whom to call for advice, information, and help.
- Demand prevention programs that are developmentally appropriate and ongoing. One discussion will not suffice.

Session 5

A Session for Young People

Session Overview

The urgent issues of child abuse must be addressed with all community members, especially children and teenagers. Young people need realistic tools that will carry them through difficult situations and empower them to take a positive stand for themselves and one another. In this session the participants will learn the warning signs that signal trouble in a potentially abusive relationship. The activities included will build both awareness and confidence.

Outcomes

- The learner will identify the risk factors associated with sexual abuse.
- The learner will develop a plan for responding to and supporting others in a crisis situation.
- The learner will be provided with information and tools to identify and steer away from questionable and potentially dangerous situations.

Facilitation

The facilitator's role is to allow for an open discussion where all participants share (only if they so choose). The facilitator should introduce the purpose of the session and the guidelines for the discussion. It is essential that the facilitator of this session have excellent listening skills. The facilitator should not be a member of the clergy. The presence of or cofacilitation by a professional psychologist or social worker is strongly suggested. At a minimum, a professional should be readily accessible if needed.

The facilitator must be candid and honest with the participants from the onset. The young people must be told from the start that the facilitator and the other adults present (mostly ministry volunteers) have a legal and ethical responsibility to report any alleged abuse.

The other adults present should be attentive listeners, allowing the young people to voice their feelings, thoughts, questions, and concerns as needed. A ratio of one adult for every four young people is suggested. Adults should be sporadically seated as a part of the group, although this is not a forum for them to voice their views, unless asked by the young people. Adults should be honest and respectful at all times, allowing the facilitator to function in his or her role and aiding in that role. Adults should fully understand the importance of listening.

Session at a Glance

- Just the Facts (20 minutes)
- How Do I Protect Myself? (25 minutes)
- Where Do We Go from Here? (25 minutes)
- Prayer Service: You Know Me (10 minutes)

Session Content

Just the Facts (20 minutes)

Preparation

Gather the following items:

- ☐ newsprint or poster board and markers
- ☐ pens or pencils, one for each participant
- ☐ a Bible
- ☐ copies of handout 1, " Quiz Time," one for each participant
- ☐ copies of handout 7, "Discussion Starters," one for each participant
- ☐ copies of resource 4, "Prayer Card," one for each participant
- ☐ a recording of reflective instrumental music and the appropriate equipment to play it (optional)

- Copy onto cardstock resource 5, "Four Steps to Creating a Safe and Sacred Place." Make enough copies so that when you cut the cards apart there will be enough for each participant to have one.
- On a sheet of newsprint, write the following statements:
  - Practice asking questions.
  - Trust your instincts.
  - Be clear about what you want and need.
  - Get involved.
- Ask for a volunteer to proclaim the Scripture passage during the closing prayer.

1. Welcome the participants and provide a brief overview of the session. Then distribute to each participant a copy of handout 1 and a pen or pencil. Invite the participants to take a few minutes to complete the handout on their own. Allow about 5 to 7 minutes for them to do this.

2. When everyone has completed the quiz, review each question and provide the participants with the correct answers and additional information as noted below:

- Can a person be sexually abused without being touched?
  - **Answer.** Yes. In reality, sexual abuse can take on various forms. It can be actions involving sexual intercourse to fondling under or over the clothes to the sexual exploitation of children where no direct physical action is perpetrated but where they are in the presence of someone who is clearly becoming sexually aroused by their presence. For example, a perpetrator might expose a child to pornography while watching to see what the child does in response to this exploitation, or a perpetrator might take photos of a naked child for personal sexual stimulation.
- What percentage of the time does a victim of sexual abuse know his or her abuser?
  - **Answer.** 90 percent. Sexual abuse happens most often with people who know the victim. Stranger abuse is fairly rare. Abuse also happens in familiar places. Abusers are most often fathers, stepfathers, siblings, aunts, uncles, baby-sitters, caretakers, or supervisors. Normally the victim of sexual abuse knows his or her abuser.
- Who is the most common sex offender?
  - **Answer.** A white married male. Perpetrators of sexual abuse usually know their victims. Most often, sex offenders are white married males, but sex offenders can be found in every socioeconomic classification, every race, every sexual orientation, and every description. Contrary to the impression given by the media, sexual offenders are also found in every religious background.

- What is a person called who is attracted sexually to a child between the ages of fourteen and eighteen?
  - **Answer.** An ephebophile. An ephebophile is an individual who is attracted sexually to a pubertal child or adolescent in the age range of fourteen to eighteen. Ephebophiles tend to have significantly fewer victims and seem less fixated than pedophiles.
- What is the percentage of priests in the United States who are reported sex offenders?
  - **Answer.** 0.2 percent to 4 percent in the low range; 4 percent to 8 percent in the high range. The Center for Applied Research in the Apostolate at Georgetown University estimates the total number of priests in the United States to be about 47,000. It estimates that 79 percent of these priests are diocesan, with the remaining 21 percent being religious order priests. Some estimate that 0.2 percent to 4 percent, or minimally between 100 and 2,000 priests, are sex offenders.
- Under Church law can a priest choose or be forced to resign from being a priest as a result of his sexual offenses?
  - **Answer.** No. Theology surrounding the priesthood changed after the Council of Trent in the sixteenth century. The priest's very being was defined as forever changed as a result of simply being ordained into the "order" of "priest." In this Catholic framework, ordination to the priesthood is such a significant and altering event that even if a priest decides to renounce his duties, he can never technically resign from being a priest. "He cannot become a layman again in the strict sense, because the character imprinted by ordination is forever"[6] (*CCC*, no. 1583). In being ordained, the priest, as stated in Hebrews 5:6, is considered "a priest forever according to the order of Melchizedek."
- Do most children readily tell an adult, usually a parent, when something serious like sexual abuse happens to them?
  - **Answer.** No. Children frequently do not tell about being sexually abused, especially if the abuser is a member of the family. Those who have broken their silence are very often not believed as children or as adults. Abused children often struggle with the thought that they must be very bad for God to allow the abuse to happen in the first place.
- Why is abuse not often reported immediately?
  - **Answer.** There are often no witnesses. The key to understanding why sexual abuse is not reported immediately is recognizing that so often the abuse happens in a secluded place. The abuser most often is someone who has power and influence over the child and who has used that power and influence to both groom and silence the child. Victims often want to tell and want to have the abuse stopped. As children, victims do not possess the mental capacity

to break away from the power of their abuser to report what is happening.

- Are most offenders prosecuted and punished?
  - **Answer.** No. Only a few of those who commit sexual assaults are apprehended and convicted for their crimes. Most convicted sex offenders are eventually released into the community under probation or parole supervision.
- Of those who abuse, how many were abused themselves?
  - **Answer.** 30 percent. Most sex offenders were not sexually assaulted as children, and most children who are sexually assaulted do not sexually assault others. Not all abusers are acting out of revenge for their past victimization. Adolescent sex offenders do not always become adult offenders. Factors that may influence a victim to become an abuser include when the abuse happened, what kind of treatment the victim received, how the family reacted to the abuse, how many times the abuse took place, and what kind of abuse was inflicted on the victim.

3. Ask the participants the following questions:

- What surprised you in this activity?
- Is there anything in the quiz that is not surprising to you or that you already knew?
- How realistic do you think these facts are?

How Do I Protect Myself? (25 minutes)

1. Provide each participant with a copy of handout 7. Allow 5 minutes for the participants to complete the handout on their own.

2. Divide the large group into smaller groups of four to six. Be sure to place an adult facilitator in each group. The facilitator will not need to give any information or plan any discussion. The facilitator's role should be only to listen, to ensure that the conversation stays focused on the topic assigned, to answer questions of clarification that may arise, and to ensure that each young person in the group has an opportunity to speak. Take a few minutes with the participants to explain the role of the adults for this activity.

3. Tell the groups they will have 10 minutes to share with their small group their responses to each section of the handout. Be sure to share the following points:

- Talking about sexual abuse can be awkward and uncomfortable. You will want to remember that fact as you begin your discussions.
- There is no right or wrong answer to any of the questions. The purpose of the discussion is to give voice to your own concerns, as well

as to listen to the thoughts and concerns of others in hopes of better understanding and becoming more aware of the issues.

- In your discussion be sure to include responses to these questions:
  - Which words did you choose to describe your feeling about discussing sexual abuse? Why do you think you feel this way?
  - What did you rate highest? lowest? What is your reasoning for the rating choices that you made?

Check in with the groups after 10 minutes, and allow for additional time if needed.

4. Gather the participants back in a large group, and ask for a sampling of answers from each small group. Use the following points below to guide you:

- Read each word from the first section of the handout, asking for a show of hands from those who chose each one.
- Invite a sampling of reasons why a particular word was chosen.
- Find out which asset was rated highest among the group.
- Ask the participants what they think they could do to improve the quality of the assets they chose (regardless of how they were rated).
- Ask for a sampling of responses to each of the five sentence starters on the handout. Add appropriate comments and clarifications where necessary.
- Remind the participants that none of these answers is right or wrong but that the opportunity to speak their thoughts and feelings in a safe and trusting place and to listen to the concerns of others is a valuable tool in working together as a community.

Where Do We Go from Here? (25 minutes)

1. Invite the participants to gather into their small groups from the previous activity. Present the following helpful hints to the group, adding your own words and examples where appropriate. You may wish to refer to the newsprint you have posted, which highlights these hints.

- Nothing we will learn in these sessions will prevent all young people from ever being harmed in any way. However, there are some tools and tips we can practice that will be beneficial in creating safe and sacred places and that will offer the coping skills necessary to move through a time of crisis.
- Crisis can touch our lives in the form of something such as a failing grade on a test or in a class, a broken friendship, minor mistakes or accidents, or something more serious such as a devastating accident or illness, or even physical, emotional, or sexual abuse. Here are some tips and tools you will want to keep in mind for staying safe and for dealing with tough times:

- **Practice asking questions.** Spend one entire day thinking of a question for everything you do in that day. Do not rule out any questions. Try to think of everything, from how orange juice is squeezed from oranges to why math was created, from whether you should believe a rumor you heard to how a person is affected by participating in extra-curricular activities. After an entire day of asking questions, you will find that you do not need to ask questions about everything all the time, but certainly you take some things for granted and blindly accept as truth yet do not always know why you accept them. There is often more information to be gained than what you have immediately available to you. Practicing asking questions will get you into the habit of seeking all available resources to help you learn more about something, a habit that will be especially beneficial when a serious situation arises and you need to make an informed decision.
- **Trust your instincts.** As you mature into young adulthood, you are becoming more and more aware of the opportunities to make choices for yourself. Along with this opportunity comes the responsibility to surround yourself with people—peers and adults—who will help guide you in making healthy choices. Through prayer and conversation, you can learn about the ways your decisions impact other people—either positively or negatively. You must also trust in the gifts God has given you. Your intuition alerts you when something is not right, your complex mind makes sense of a complicated situation, and your spiritual connection with God provides you the perseverance and strength to carry through difficult times. Practice trusting your feelings by discussing how you feel about something with another person you trust—a parent, sibling, friend, or significant adult. Use journaling to voice your thoughts on paper, and allow the tool of writing to help you unfold and clarify your daily thoughts.
- **Be clear about what you want and need.** How simple is it to ask for a new game, a new bike, a new car, or new clothes for your birthday or as a holiday gift? What if you were able to voice your internal needs and wants just as clearly and easily? It is okay to tell someone that you feel uncomfortable or want to get out of a situation because it doesn't feel right, whether the situation is lying, stealing, gossiping, or putting someone down. You don't have to do something that goes against what you believe is right just because someone else says you should—even if that someone is an adult. Practice being clear about what you need to be healthy in everyday life situations—how much sleep you need, communicating how you are feeling, wanting to have time alone, or needing help with homework. Communicating what you need has nothing

to do with being selfish. In fact, it is self-care to think about and to articulate what your body, mind, and soul need to stay healthy and happy. Look to the significant adults in your life, such as your parents, teachers, or trusted family and friends, to help you balance the difference between need and greed.

- **Get involved.** Being involved in the community does not have anything to do with being popular or being the most active or voted the friendliest or most outgoing. Do not limit yourself because you don't think you deserve to be an active community member. Educate yourself about the different ways you can be involved in the community. Find something that is interesting to you. Take piano lessons outside of school, meet your neighbors, volunteer at a local shelter, baby-sit for family and friends, walk in a benefit race, teach Bible stories to children at your church, tutor peers, or participate in a team or club. Choose something that inspires you or is interesting to you. Being involved serves two main purposes: (1) you get to know other teens and adults who can potentially support you and whom you can potentially trust, and (2) you build your own character, set examples for others, and gain insight into who you are and who you want to be. Community involvement gives you an opportunity to think about your future and your goals.

- Ask the participants if they have any additional tips or ideas to offer. Allow for some discussion if time permits.

2. Tell the participants that each small group is to create an advertisement for one of the tips they have just heard. You will need to provide each group with a sheet of newsprint or a poster board and several markers. You will also need to assign each group one of the four tips presented in step 1. It is okay if several groups are assigned the same tip.

3. Tell the groups to imagine they are at a baseball game, riding in a car, watching pre-movie commercials, surfing the Internet, or reading a magazine. They should create an advertisement for that place or space. You can assign one of those locations to each small group, or you can invite the groups to choose a different location they would like to create an advertisement for. Ask them to create an advertisement that might be found in the location they have chosen. Remind the groups that their advertisement should be engaging, interesting, and informative and that it should make a viewer want to buy the product or service they are promoting. Invite the groups to imagine how they could make their viewers want to have this "product." To make the activity more challenging, tell the groups that the other groups will judge their advertisements for effectiveness and that there will be prizes awarded to the winning advertisements. Give the groups 10 minutes to complete the assigned task.

4. Invite each group to present to the large group the advertisement they have created. Add comments and suggestions where necessary. Consider posting the advertisements in a visible location for other parishioners or other "safe and sacred" participants to see.

5. Distribute to each participant a copy of the cards you have made from resource 5. Suggest that each participant place the card in an accessible and visible location, such as a wallet, purse, bathroom mirror, nightstand, or school locker.

Prayer Service: You Know Me (10 minutes)

1. Invite the volunteer you have selected to come forward to proclaim Jeremiah 29:11–12. Allow a few moments of silence after the reading.

2. Share the following points with the participants:

- Although many things in life may challenge us, God has great things in mind for each of us.
- God knew us even before we were born and desires for us to follow God's lead and be guided by God's love.
- God's plans for each of us involve growing spiritually, seeking goodness, and trusting in God's all-knowing power.
- With God's guidance we can persevere through difficult situations.

3. Distribute a copy of resource 4 and a pen or pencil to each participant. Invite the participants to prayerfully respond to the sentence starters. Remind them that this activity is for personal reflection and that they are not to discuss with others or work in groups during this time. You may wish to play some reflective instrumental music to encourage a quiet atmosphere. Allow 5 to 10 minutes, depending on the needs of the group.

4. Conclude by inviting the participants to pray the closing prayer together:

> Lord, you have created me with specific thoughts, ideas, and characteristics. You know everything about me. You know who I am and who I will become. You have plans for me that are wonderful, plans that I might not even be able to imagine for myself. Help me to trust in your guidance, Lord. Help me to believe that I don't

have to do anything by myself. Help me to remember that you are ever present, all-knowing, and completely loving. Grant me the gifts I need to believe in myself. When I feel discouraged, remind me that I am capable. When I feel lonely, bring friends and family to support me. When I am confused, show me the right path to follow. When I doubt the future, enlighten me to trust in your creative plans. I ask all this with a humble heart and with much gratitude. Amen.

Discussion Starters

I think talking about sexual abuse is (circle one word) . . .

scary	uncomfortable	gross	important
necessary	helpful	pointless	

Rank the assets that you need to be a healthy and happy teenager:

_____ caring adults and parents
_____ patience
_____ a relationship with God
_____ a good job
_____ money
_____ friends
_____ trust
_____ an education

If a friend told me that he or she had been sexually abused as a child, I would . . .

If someone asked me how I felt about talking to my parents about sex, I would say . . .

If I were in a situation with someone where I felt uncomfortable and wanted to get out of the situation for my safety, I could say or tell the person . . .

If that person were an adult, I would . . .

If someone in my community were accused of sexually abusing someone, I would feel . . .

Prayer Card

For surely I know the plans I have for you, says the LORD, plans for your welfare and not for harm, to give you a future with hope. Then when you call upon me and come and pray to me, I will hear you. (Jer. 29:11–12)

Some of my hopes and dreams are . . .

A person who reminds me to trust God's goodness is . . .

Three words that encourage me are . . .

Say to yourself: "God loves me and knows me and believes in me."

Lord, you have created me with specific thoughts, ideas, and characteristics. You know everything about me. You know who I am and who I will become. You have plans for me that are wonderful, plans that I might not even be able to imagine for myself. Help me to trust in your guidance, Lord. Help me to believe that I don't have to do anything by myself. Help me to remember that you are ever present, all-knowing, and completely loving. Grant me the gifts I need to believe in myself. When I feel discouraged, remind me that I am capable. When I feel lonely, bring friends and family to support me. When I am confused, show me the right path to follow. When I doubt the future, enlighten me to trust in your creative plans. I ask all this with a humble heart and with much gratitude. Amen.

For surely I know the plans I have for you, says the LORD, plans for your welfare and not for harm, to give you a future with hope. Then when you call upon me and come and pray to me, I will hear you. (Jer. 29:11–12)

Some of my hopes and dreams are . . .

A person who reminds me to trust God's goodness is . . .

Three words that encourage me are . . .

Say to yourself: "God loves me and knows me and believes in me."

Lord, you have created me with specific thoughts, ideas, and characteristics. You know everything about me. You know who I am and who I will become. You have plans for me that are wonderful, plans that I might not even be able to imagine for myself. Help me to trust in your guidance, Lord. Help me to believe that I don't have to do anything by myself. Help me to remember that you are ever present, all-knowing, and completely loving. Grant me the gifts I need to believe in myself. When I feel discouraged, remind me that I am capable. When I feel lonely, bring friends and family to support me. When I am confused, show me the right path to follow. When I doubt the future, enlighten me to trust in your creative plans. I ask all this with a humble heart and with much gratitude. Amen.

Four Steps to Creating a Safe and Sacred Place

- Practice asking questions.
- Trust your instincts.
- Be clear about what you want and need.
- Get involved.

- Practice asking questions.
- Trust your instincts.
- Be clear about what you want and need.
- Get involved.

- Practice asking questions.
- Trust your instincts.
- Be clear about what you want and need.
- Get involved.

- Practice asking questions.
- Trust your instincts.
- Be clear about what you want and need.
- Get involved.

- Practice asking questions.
- Trust your instincts.
- Be clear about what you want and need.
- Get involved.

- Practice asking questions.
- Trust your instincts.
- Be clear about what you want and need.
- Get involved.

- Practice asking questions.
- Trust your instincts.
- Be clear about what you want and need.
- Get involved.

- Practice asking questions.
- Trust your instincts.
- Be clear about what you want and need.
- Get involved.

- Practice asking questions.
- Trust your instincts.
- Be clear about what you want and need.
- Get involved.

A Session for Young People

Session Overview

Adolescents live in the balance between childhood and adulthood. Constant changes and physical, emotional, and spiritual development cause confusion and clarity, inconsistency and inspiration, hope and hopelessness. Caring adults are responsible to guide teenagers into adulthood, empowering them with confidence, security, and wisdom. With this growth and guidance comes the opportunity to recognize the gifts of adolescents that can help guide younger children. Teenagers can choose to influence children negatively, just as easily as they can choose to influence children positively. The activities in this session will encourage young people to continue to journey into adulthood in healthy and safe ways and with the continued support of caring adults.

Outcomes

- The learner will be aware of the tools, resources, and guidance that are available to him or her to help create a safe and sacred community.

- The learner will discuss the importance of preventing sexual abuse.
- The learner will identify ways that young people can be role models for younger children and develop confidence in setting an example.

Facilitation

The facilitator's role is to allow for an open discussion in which all the participants share (only if they so choose). The facilitator should introduce the purpose of the session and the guidelines for the discussion. It is essential that the facilitator of this session have excellent listening skills. The facilitator should not be a member of the clergy. The presence of or cofacilitation by a professional psychologist or social worker is strongly suggested. At a minimum, a professional should be readily accessible if needed.

The facilitator should be candid and honest with the participants from the onset. The young people must be told from the start that all the adults present (the facilitator and youth ministry volunteers) have a legal and ethical responsibility to report any alleged abuse.

The youth ministry volunteers who are present should be attentive listeners, allowing the young people to voice their feelings, thoughts, questions, and concerns as needed. A ratio of one adult for every four young people is suggested. Adults should be sporadically seated as a part of the group, although this is not a forum for them to voice their views, unless asked by the young people. Adults should be honest and respectful at all times, allowing the facilitator to function in his or her role and aiding in that role. Adults should fully understand the importance of listening.

Adult Participation

Consider inviting a variety of members from the faith community to meet and greet the young people prior to the session in a reception-style activity. The reception does not have to include discussion about abuse but should include opportunities for adults and young people to meet one another in a neutral and safe place. The adults and young people gathered should be told that the gathering is a part of a program intended to create safe and sacred places and to foster an open and aware community. It is important that adults not be tricked into meeting the young people of the faith community; they should see the value and reason for the gathering. The adults at the reception should include people who support the young people in the parish but may not have the occasion to work with or meet them directly. These adults might include members of the altar society, Knights of Columbus, prayer groups, or the parish council; non-faculty school staff; school benefactors and board members; diocesan staff members, including the bishop, religious community members, and various others members; and groups who would like to become more familiar with the work and benefits of the youth ministry programming.

Session at a Glance

- Seeking Community Support (30 minutes)
- Make Us Living Symbols (30 minutes)
- Praying Our Concerns (15 minutes)

Session Content

Preparation

Gather the following items:

- ☐ newsprint and markers
- ☐ blank sheets of paper, one for each participant
- ☐ pens or pencils, one for each participant

- Choose a representative from a local agency to speak to the issues of teen development, preventing sexual abuse, healing from sexual abuse, keeping your body and mind safe, or other related topics. Choose a speaker who relates well to young people, has realistic information to share, and will be open and honest with the participants. Resource 6, "Suggested Speaker Notes (1)," provides additional information, including a suggested outline for the presentation. Be sure to provide the speaker with the session notes well in advance so that she or he can prepare and be clear on expectations and needs. You may want to consider extending the session time frame and inviting a panel of speakers to cover different aspects relating to the session program.
- Write the following questions on a sheet of newsprint and post it where all the participants will be able to see it:
  - What are two things from the presentation that struck you or will stick with you?
  - How will the resources provided by the speaker or his or her agency or profession be beneficial to our community?
  - Name at least three benefits.
  - What will you do with the information that you have gained in these sessions and this presentation?
- You will need to obtain a copy of your parish community's general intercessions from the three previous Sunday liturgies.

Seeking Community Support (30 minutes)

1. Welcome the participants and provide a brief overview of the session. Be sure to note that a speaker will be joining the session. Let them know there will be time to discuss with the speaker and with one another what they are about to hear in the presentation.

2. Introduce the speaker and allow 10 to 15 minutes for him or her to present using the suggested outline noted on resource 6. When the speaker has concluded, thank her or him for joining the session and then invite the speaker to stay while the participants discuss what they heard.

3. Divide the large into small groups of five to seven. Be sure to assign an adult facilitator to each group. The facilitator's role is to listen, to ensure that the conversation stays focused on the topic assigned, to answer questions of clarification in the small group, and to ensure that each young person in the group has an opportunity to speak. Take a few minutes to share with the participants the role of the adults for this activity. Be sure the adults understand their role well. It is important to give the young people a safe place to speak without judgment or unnecessary interruption.

Then ask the groups to discuss their responses to the questions you posted on newsprint before the session. If the speaker has provided you with suggested discussion questions, use the speaker's questions in addition to or in place of these:

- What are two things from the presentation that struck you or will stick with you?
- How will the resources provided by the speaker or his or her agency or profession be beneficial to our community?
- Name at least three benefits.
- What will you do with the information that you have gained in these sessions and this presentation?

Allow ample time for the groups to discuss.

4. Gather the participants into a large group and invite a few participants to share their responses or thoughts.

Make Us Living Symbols (30 minutes)

1. Share the following points with the participants:

- Although all young people deserve to be cared for and protected by the adults in the community, teenagers also have a unique opportunity to care for and be an example to those who are younger.

- Some teenagers have younger siblings or cousins. Teenagers are often called upon to serve the faith community through programs such as grade school mentoring or vacation Bible school.
- Many teenagers volunteer in the community, through their school or church, in service agencies that work with and for children.
- Regardless of the amount of involvement, the reality is that young children look up to teenagers.
- Teenagers have the skills and capabilities to be loving, supportive, and encouraging to young children.
- Because young children look up to them and admire them, teenagers also have a responsibility to learn about and practice critical thinking in how they act and in the choices they make.
- There is no doubt that teenagers' actions and words are often closely watched and heard by impressionable children.
- Teenagers have a great opportunity to educate young children about safety matters and can play a significant role in creating and maintaining safe and sacred environments for all community members.

2. Invite the participants to gather once again in their small groups. Provide each group with a sheet of newsprint and a few markers. Ask the participants to put their minds together to name some of the ways they make positive impressions on those who are younger. Allow a few minutes for some initial discussion in the groups.

3. Ask the groups to create a list of ten things that all children should know about as they grow up in order to become healthy teens and healthy adults. To make the process a little more challenging or creative, assign a specific title to each group's list. Use the following, or create your own:

- Top 10 Ways for Teens to Show Kids They Care
- Top 10 Words of Encouragement for Kids
- Top 10 Words That Describe Life as a Teenager
- Top 10 Scripture Verses That Inspire Teens
- Top 10 Words of Advice for Kids to Grow into Healthy and Hopeful Teens
- Top 10 Ways Teenagers Can Positively Influence the Lives of Kids

Allow the groups 10 to 15 minutes to create their lists. Be sure to visit each group while they are working to ensure that they understand the process, to encourage their work, and to see whether they need any further instructions or help.

4. Ask for a representative from each small group to present the list to the large group. Remind participants to look closely at other groups' lists and to listen for similarities between lists.

5. After each group has presented, ask the participants to choose one or two ideas they could incorporate into their interactions with children. Invite a few participants to offer their thoughts about an action plan. Consider hanging the lists in a place where teenagers will see them often and be reminded of their opportunity to be role models for young children.

Praying Our Concerns (15 minutes)

1. Read aloud the general intercessions you gathered prior to the session. Allow a few moments of silence after each petition. Once you have read all the intercessions, share the following points with the participants:

- Each of the intercessions I just read is an example of a prayer petition that we pray as a community.
- Recall that during Sunday liturgy we pray many different petitions, including prayers for world leaders, Church leaders, and community leaders; those who are lost, forgotten, or who feel hopeless; those who are sick; and the dying and the dead. We say prayers for guidance, peace, and in gratitude; prayers for the future and for perseverance; and prayers of thanksgiving for gifts given.
- Petitions, or intercessions, are the prayers of a community gathered to seek God's guidance and help.
- When we address God in petition, our prayers are not singular; they are multiplied over and over by the many members of the community who also seek God's help.

2. Tell the participants they will have an opportunity to create intercessions that speak to what they have learned in these sessions. As they create their own petitions, ask them to indicate what they would like to offer or ask God. Remind the participants that each petition should speak not only to their own concerns but also to the concerns of the entire community.

3. Divide the large group into small groups of three. Give each small group a sheet of paper and a pen or pencil. Instruct each group to write a petition patterned after what they have learned about petitions from the examples you read. Their petition should be about a specific need or issue that you assign to them and should relate to the information they have gained and discussed in the sessions about preventing sexual abuse. Assign one of the following needs or issues to each small group. Because of the number of groups, it is possible that a need or issue will be assigned to more than one group.

- wisdom
- belief
- trust
- hope
- courage
- guidance
- healing
- forgiveness
- gratitude
- victims
- abusers
- setting an example

Allow 5 to 7 minutes for each group to create a petition with their assigned focus. Visit each group while they are working to see whether they can use help with wording or need further guidance.

4. Gather the participants back into the large group. Invite each group to voice their petitions out loud, and ask the other participants to respond with one of the following phrases:

- "Lord, hear our prayer."
- "Giver of life, hear our prayer."
- "God, our protector, hear our prayer."
- "Merciful God, hear us."

You might also choose a response that the group agrees upon. In your response be sure to remember to address the community (our, us), God (Lord, Redeemer), and listening (hear, receive).

5. Conclude by inviting the participants to join in praying the Lord's Prayer.

Variation

Inquire about using the participants' authored petitions with regularly scheduled liturgies. These prayers can be used in a particular liturgy, or they can be intermingled over the course of several weeks. Invite a group of adolescent participants to meet with the liturgist or other liturgy planner to learn about the process of preparing petitions for the liturgies. The liturgist might also want to ask questions to get a clear picture of what the teens are hoping to voice within the community's prayer.

Suggested Speaker Notes (1)

Thank you for agreeing to speak to our youth community about the work that you do, its impact on the community, and the effort to create safe places for children. In your presentation please be sure to include the points listed below. The young people are expecting to hear this information and will use the information you give them as part of a follow-up discussion. You will find their discussion questions below for your reference. You will have 15 to 20 minutes to present your material.

Suggested Speaker Outline

- Tell about who you are and the work you do in the community.
- Give details about how your work or service impacts the community.
- Give a specific example or story of someone who has benefited from the work of your agency or profession.
- Describe how you feel teens can use the information offered by your agency or profession.
- Give any specific information or facts your listeners will find helpful in creating a complete picture of the message you are trying to convey.
- Please add any other information you think is useful in helping teens have a part in fostering safe environments for themselves and others.

Do you have any ideas for discussion questions that the participants can use after your presentation to enhance its message?

Follow-Up Discussion Questions

- What are two things from the presentation that struck you or will stick with you?
- How will the resources provided by the speaker or his or her agency or profession be beneficial to our community? Name at least three benefits.
- What will you do with the information that you have gained in these sessions and this presentation?

A Listening Session for Young People

Session Overview

The purpose of this session is to allow the young people in a school or parish to gather in a safe and trusting place to voice their feelings, thoughts, and concerns when Church scandal occurs. This session is not for rallying people's criticisms, views, or protests. It is not for persuading others toward a particular view or opinion. It is strictly a listening session for feelings and concerns to be expressed and heard, and for the sharing or clarification of facts. This session creates a safe place for the young people to name the feelings that can be stepping stones in the process of healing for the individual and for the community.

Outcomes

- The learner will be offered the chance to share feelings, thoughts, and concerns.
- The learner will pray for the healing of the victims and those who suffer any type of abuse as well as for those who have brought harm against another through any kind of abuse.

- The learner will discuss with others the possible means for healing and reconciliation of members within the parish community who suffer and struggle in this time of pain.

Facilitation

The facilitator's role is to allow for an open discussion where all the participants share (only if they so choose). The facilitator should introduce the purpose of the session and the guidelines for the discussion. It is essential that the facilitator of this session have excellent listening skills. The facilitator should not be a member of the clergy. The presence of or cofacilitation by a professional psychologist or social worker is strongly suggested. At a minimum, a professional should be readily accessible if needed.

Other adults who are present (youth ministry volunteers) should be attentive listeners, allowing the young people to voice their feelings, thoughts, and concerns as needed. The adults may also report or clarify the facts. Adults should be sporadically seated as a part of the circle, although this is not a forum for them to voice their views, unless asked by the young people. Adults should be honest and respectful at all times, allowing the facilitator to function in his or her role and aiding in that role. The facilitator may wish to consider inviting at least one member of the parish pastoral staff, all parish youth ministry staff, and at least one of the parish priests to attend. If the parish has a counselor or social worker, the facilitator may want to invite him or her as well. Again, strong attention must be given to the voice of the young people and to the facilitator's ability to monitor unasked-for adult responses. Adults should fully understand the importance of listening.

Session at a Glance

- Welcome (5 minutes)
- Gathering Prayer (5 minutes)
- Introduction of Procedures and Discussion Guidelines (5 minutes)
- "I Feel" Statements and Group Sharing (50 minutes)
- Summary of the Discussion (15 minutes)
- Closing Prayer (10 minutes)

Session Content

Preparation

Gather the following items:

- ☐ 3-by-5-inch index cards, one for each participant
- ☐ pens or pencils, one for each participant
- ☐ newsprint and markers
- ☐ a Bible
- ☐ hymnals or worship aids with printed music, one for each participant
- ☐ copies of any handouts or contact information you wish to provide

- You will need to select one of the two ritual actions suggested in the closing prayer and then gather the necessary supplies.
- Ask for one volunteer to proclaim the Scripture reading and another to offer the prayers of intercession during the closing prayer.
- You will want to have a music leader available or the necessary music and equipment (recorded music and a CD or tape player) if a music leader is not present.
- Select a closing song. You might choose from these:
  - "Canticle of the Turning," by Rory Cooney, in *Gather Comprehensive* (Chicago: GIA Publications)
  - "Christ, Be Our Light," by Bernadette Farrell, in *Today's Missal Music Issue* (Portland, OR: Oregon Catholic Press)
  - "Confitemini Domino/Come and Fill," by Jacques Berthier/Taizé Community, in *Gather Comprehensive* (Chicago: GIA Publications)
  - "God of Day and God of Darkness," by Marty Haugen, in *Gather Comprehensive* (Chicago: GIA Publications)
  - "Jesus, Heal Us," by David Haas, in *Gather Comprehensive* (Chicago: GIA Publications)
  - "Remember Your Love," by D. Ducote, G. Daigle, and M. Balhoff, in *Today's Missal Music Issue* (Portland, OR: Oregon Catholic Press)
- You will want to ensure that the gathering space provides an atmosphere of comfort, safety, and trust. Invite the young people and adults to sit in a circle, either on chairs or on the floor, so that they are all at the same eye level.

Welcome (5 minutes)

1. Begin the session by stating the purpose for the gathering. Explain that an atmosphere of respect for all feelings, thoughts, and opinions must be maintained. Reassure the young people that confidentiality will also be respected. Introduce the facilitator and explain her or his role. (If you are serving as the facilitator, you will want to provide the participants with a bit of background about your role in the community.) Then introduce the additional adults or team members who are present.

Gathering Prayer (5 minutes)

1. Distribute a hymnal or worship aid to each participant. Begin by inviting the participants to take a moment of silence, and then offer the following prayer:

Leader: In the name of the Father and of the Son and of the Holy Spirit. The Lord be with you.

All: And also with you.

Leader: God, our Creator, we ask you to give us hope in the midst of discouragement, perseverance in our frustration, and continuous reminders of your love throughout this difficult time. May we be of support to one another, always attentive and caring. Send us your Spirit of wisdom and guidance. Be at our side now and always. We ask this in the name of Jesus, the Lord. Amen.

Introduction of Procedures and Discussion Guidelines (5 minutes)

1. Share with participants the following guidelines for the discussion:

- Each person is entitled to share his or her thoughts or feelings. If you do not wish to share aloud, that is okay.
- The goal is not to try to persuade others toward a particular view or opinion. We are here to express and hear concerns and to share and clarify facts.
- It is very important that we offer our full attention to each person who speaks.
- What is shared among us will be kept among us. However, any indication or sharing of past or current misconduct or abuse must be reported to local authorities. If anyone shares that she or he is a victim or an offender, the adults are required by law and Church policy to report such abuse.
- We are not here to judge others or the Church. We are here to share our thoughts and feelings and to respond to questions and needs when appropriate.
- This is a sharing time for you, the young people of the community. The adults who are present are here to support and encourage good dialogue and process. They are here to listen and to respond only when asked to do so.

"I Feel" Statements and Group Sharing (50 minutes)

1. Distribute to each participant an index card and a pen or pencil. Explain that using an "I feel" statement will allow each participant to focus on feelings and thoughts rather than on complaints or criticisms.

2. Invite the young people to write on the index card the following sentence, leaving a blank space where indicated:

- "I feel ___________ when ___________ because ___________."

You may wish to post the above statement on newsprint for easy reference throughout this process.

3. Invite the participants to take a few minutes to collect their thoughts and then write down their feelings (first blank), the situations that are causing the feelings (second blank), and the reason for their feelings about the situation (third blank). Make sure they do *not* put their name on their cards. You may wish to offer an example such as:

- "I feel disappointed when someone has caused harm in our community because I trusted him or her." Give the participants about 5 minutes to complete the "I feel" statement on their index cards.

4. Collect all the cards and shuffle them. Then redistribute the cards, one card to each participant. Once all the young people have a card, ask for a volunteer to read the card she or he has chosen. Allow ample time for feedback or clarification after each card is read. Continue with this process until each card has been read and discussed.

Summary of the Discussion (15 minutes)

1. Conduct a brief summation of what has been shared. Allow all the participants the opportunity to voice what they heard, one piece of information at a time. Suggest that the young people use the phrase "Tonight I heard . . ." to share what they learned. You may wish to note each comment on newsprint. Be sure that everyone who wishes to share has an opportunity to do so.

2. Brainstorm with the participants some next-step possibilities. For example, the group may decide to meet again to revisit feelings and the process of healing, or they may brainstorm concrete, proactive ways to grow from the situation.

Closing Prayer (10 minutes)

1. Invite the chosen volunteer to come forward to proclaim 2 Corinthians 4:5–12. Allow a few moments of silence to follow, and then respond with Psalm 91, either spoken, sung, or played from a recording.

2. Implement one of the following ritual actions:

Options for Ritual Actions

Paper chain. Use slips of paper instead of 3-by-5-inch cards for the comments. Ask each young person to hold, as in prayer, the statement that he or she read. Explain that each person will be gluing the ends of their slip together to form a circular link. One at a time, invite each person to bring the slip of paper forward. Create a paper chain by looping each slip of paper into the previous one and gluing the ends together. Connecting the links of the chain can symbolize that even in our brokenness we are called to be the one Body of Christ.

A blessing with oil. Oil, an ancient, historical symbol of healing and anointing, can be a powerful agent within the context of prayer. Note that the oil used should not be sacramental, as sacramental oil is reserved strictly for the sacraments of Baptism, Confirmation, Anointing of the Sick, and Holy Orders. You may use any plain olive oil. Provide a brief explanation of the biblical accounts in which oil is used as a sign of healing, of being called to ministerial leadership, of being anointed as prophet, to speak the truth courageously in a world that does not want to hear. Follow the anointing with a blessing of hands. With the oil, place the sign of the cross on the back of the hands, symbolizing the work of our hands as healing agents for our communities and for our world.

As another option, again begin with an explanation of oil as a symbol and its ritual uses. Collect the 3-by-5-inch cards from the session and place them in a glass bowl. Pour the oil over them, and continue the service with the intercessions.

3. Invite the chosen volunteer to come forward to lead the participants in praying the following intercessions:

- Let us pray. Gracious and merciful God, hear the prayers of your people as we come before you with humble hearts.
- I invite each of you to respond with "Lord, help us to trust in you."
- In these dark moments of grief, pain, anger, sadness, disappointment, and frustration, we pray. . . . (all respond)
- As we struggle to move on toward greater growth but find it difficult to let go of the past, we pray. . . . (all respond)

- As we seek to find our way to truth, to wholeness, to loving others better, we pray. . . . (all respond)
- For all victims of abuse and their families, we pray. . . . (all respond)
- For perpetrators of abuse, that they may have the courage to seek the help that is needed, we pray. . . . (all respond)
- For all in authority, that they may have the wisdom and strength to make difficult yet just decisions, we pray. . . . (all respond)
- For the Church of *[name your diocese]* and the community of *[name your parish],* that we may know your healing and peace, we pray. . . . (all respond)
- We make our prayer through Christ, our Lord. Amen.

4. Conclude by offering the following prayer:

God, who dwells within, God, who is with us in good times and in bad, we turn our hearts again to you, and we proclaim: Nothing can come between us and your love for us, even if we are troubled, worried, or being persecuted; even if we lack food or clothes; even if we are being threatened or attacked. We can grow through difficult times because of this power of your love at work in our lives. For we are certain of this: neither death nor life nor angel nor principality, nothing that exists, nothing still to come, not any power, no height or depth, nor any created thing can come between us and your love, which has been made visible through Jesus. And so, we lean on you, and we offer you our thanks and praise as we make our prayer through Jesus Christ, our Lord. Amen. (Adapted from Romans 8:38)

5. Conclude by inviting the participants to join in singing the closing song you have selected.

Session 8

An Intergenerational Session

Session Overview

This gathering is intended for young people, their parents, and ministry leaders in the community. The session is designed to encourage participants of various ages to reach out to all members of the community for support, encouragement, and accountability. The individual sessions provided prior to this one offer the opportunity for teens and adults to learn in a comfortable setting appropriate to their age-group. This session brings a variety of age-groups together to share thoughts on an important topic: child sexual abuse. The combined gathering will help the participants recognize the responsibility everyone has to ensure the safety of children, no matter what age or role they play in the community.

Outcomes

- The learner will discuss the needs and concerns about sexual abuse from the perspective of both the young people and the adults in the community.

- The learner will evaluate the resources and tools available for reaching out to a community in crisis.
- The learner will collaborate with community members in a collective effort to create a safer and more sacred environment for young people.
- The learner will pledge to play a key role in raising awareness and support in the prevention of child abuse.

Facilitation

The facilitator's role is to allow for an open discussion in which all the participants can share (if they choose to do so). The facilitator should introduce the purpose of the session and any guidelines for the discussion. It is essential that the facilitator of this session have excellent listening skills. The facilitator should not be a member of the clergy. The presence of or cofacilitation by a professional psychologist or social worker is strongly suggested. At a minimum, a professional should be readily accessible if needed.

Session at a Glance

- Opening Activity (15 minutes)
- Nourishing Trust (20 minutes)
- Hoping with Confidence (20 minutes)
- Creating Safe and Sacred Places Together (30 minutes)
- Believing in the Power of Community (5 minutes)

Session Content

Preparation

Gather the following items:

- ☐ name tags (the sticker kind), one for each participant
- ☐ newsprint and markers
- ☐ blank sheets of paper
- ☐ pens or pencils, one for each participant
- ☐ several copies of your parish, school, or community bulletin or calendar (optional)
- ☐ copies of handout 8, "Community Pledge," one for each participant

- Gather some giveaway items or prizes. These items should be things that are meaningful to the session work and could include a Bible, a book or video on parent-teen communication, coupons for a family outing for ice cream, a video of a popular movie portraying relationships in a healthy and safe way, and so on.

- Write a letter of the alphabet on one corner of each name tag. Be sure to repeat commonly used letters such as *a, e, r, s, t,* and *m.*
- Invite a staff member from your diocese to outline in detail the plan the diocese has created to protect the children of the faith community. This staff member might be the diocesan director of youth ministry or religious education or the diocesan child protection advocate. Be sure the speaker will be comfortable addressing the mixed ages present. It is crucial that the speaker understand that he or she is invited to the group gathering as a positive and helpful advocate for the children of the Church. The diocesan speaker should not address or defend any specific personal situation or single out any person in the presentation. Be sure to invite a speaker who considers herself or himself to be an advocate for young people. Resource 7, "Suggested Speaker Notes (2)," provides additional information, including a suggested outline for the presentation. Be sure to provide the speaker with the session notes well in advance so that she or he can prepare and be clear on expectations and needs.
- As the participants enter the gathering space, invite each of them to fill out a name tag.

Opening Activity (15 minutes)

1. Welcome the participants and provide each with a blank sheet of paper and a pen or pencil. Tell them that each name tag has a letter of the alphabet on it. Each individual letter will be used to join with other participants to form a word. Instruct the group to create words using the following rules:

- You will have 6 minutes for this activity. When time begins, move around the room to find other letters that with your letter will form a word.
- You are to create only words that have something to do with preventing child abuse in the community.
- When you have found a set of letters, each person who formed the word should write down that word. For example, Katie has the letter *s* in the corner of her name tag. She finds five other participants with the letters *a, c, r, e,* and *d.* Everyone in that group of six writes the word *sacred* on the paper.
- Once you find and record a word, move along to find another word with other letters. For example, Katie will leave her group of *sacred* and find four other people (letters) to make the word *trust,* and all members in that word group will write the word *trust* on the paper.
- Continue to scramble and unscramble people (letters) until you have as many words as you can find and until time is called.

2. Announce when there is one minute remaining. At the end of the 6 minutes, call time.

3. Gather the participants together in the large group. Ask them to count the number of words on their individual lists. If a word is not obvious, the participant will need to explain to the large group how it relates to the topic. (Obvious words might include *safe, sacred, hope, trust, child,* and so on.)

4. Distribute prizes to the following participants:

- the one with the most words
- the one with the longest word
- the one with the least words
- the one with the most words with uncommon letters (such as *q, x,* or *j*)

5. Tell the participants that this silly game can actually teach us something positive about working to prevent child abuse. Be sure to mention the following points, allowing the group to add their thoughts as well:

- Each person needed the help of another to create a word.
- New possibilities and great diversity happened as words were formed.
- Being open to others and acting as community created more and more words.
- We need to be aware of those who try but simply cannot or do not have the means to help themselves (like the person with the letter *q,* who was limited in the words he or she could create).

6. Ask for a sampling of the words the participants created. Have them call out their words to the group. You may wish to note these words on newsprint. You will also want to allow for further insights to surface and be discussed.

Nourishing Trust (20 minutes)

1. Divide the large group into smaller groups of three to four. Each group should have a balanced mix of participants. For example, if your session includes parents, young people, and ministry leaders, be sure that each group has an equal number of each. Each group should choose a representative parent, young person, and ministry leader.

2. Tell the participants they will be asked a series of questions that the representatives in each small group will have the opportunity to answer. When each participant in a group is asked a question, only that person is allowed to speak or share a response, and he or she must do so within 1 minute. Other group members should talk only to clarify what the speaker has said or to encourage further explanation from the speaker. The purpose of the activity is to give the representatives an opportunity to say something about what they have gained or stand to gain from community education about abuse.

The activity will spur further discussion at a later time (after the session and at home). The 1-minute time frame allows a specific and special time for each person to voice a reaction to the previous sessions and the topic of abuse and also encourages each speaker to focus the answer and think about a response.

3. If there is more than one parent, young person, or ministry leader in each group, adjust the time to allow for each person to have an opportunity to share. Remind the participants that only the person who has been assigned a question can speak during the allotted minute. For example, when teens have been asked a question, only the teen representative in a group may speak. Other members (parents, leaders, other teens) can ask questions only to clarify or to encourage further or deeper explanation from the representative teen.

4. Allow 1 minute for each representative person to answer the following questions. If you sense that the participants need additional time to collect their thoughts before voicing them out loud, provide a pen or pencil and a sheet of paper to each participant and allow a set time period of no more than 1 minute for silent reflection after each question. Announce the questions one at a time, and call time at the end of each minute in order to move to the next question. While the questions are being answered in each group, walk around to hear some of the conversation and to remind the groups that only the one asked a question should be allowed to answer at that time.

- **Teens.** Name one valuable thing you have noticed or learned in the previous sessions about the issue of abuse that you hope other teens will take seriously.
- **Parents.** Why do parents want their children to be safe and happy?
- **Ministry leaders.** Name one thing you want to take to heart and work for regarding teens and preventing child abuse.
- **Teens.** Name one way you rely on adults (parents or ministry leaders) within the faith community.
- **Parents.** Complete this sentence: I think I, as a parent, should learn about creating safe and sacred places because . . .
- **Ministry leaders.** Name one reason why you value the contributions of teens in the faith community.

5. Share the following point with the participants:

- After all we have learned together, we must continue in conversation, continue to listen to one another, and continue to seek understanding of one another's concerns.

Hoping with Confidence (20 minutes)

1. Introduce the guest who will speak to the participants. Explain that this speaker has been asked to share some of the plans, procedures, and preventive measures that are in place in your local community.

2. If time allows, invite the participants to ask any clarifying questions they might have, or offer a time for brief discussion between the participants and the speaker. Consider the following discussion questions:

- What did you hear in the speaker's presentation that you found to be particularly significant?
- What reactions do you have to what you heard?

When the speaker has concluded, thank him or her for sharing, and extend an invitation for her or him to stay with the group for the remaining planning, pledge, and prayer activities.

Creating Safe and Sacred Places Together (30 minutes)

1. Remind the group of the following:

- We have spent some time during our previous sessions talking about the discomfort of discussing and addressing the topic of sexual abuse. We have faced a difficult issue. Although we have accomplished a lot, we are not yet finished. Preventing sexual abuse requires commitment, prayer, and consistent effort on the part of the community.

2. Invite the participants to consider the following question:

- Were it not for fear, what would I want to do to stop or prevent abuse of someone in our community?

Allow some time for the participants to ponder this question in silence.

3. Then share the following points with the participants:

- Fear is but one obstacle that might keep us from moving forward or accomplishing something.
- Maybe something else holds us back sometimes or keeps us silent.
- We could ask the same question and replace the word *fear* with *embarrassment, shame, mistrust,* or *doubt.*

- Even fear can take on many forms—fear of speaking out, fear of being ignored, fear of being talked about, and so on. Fear can immobilize us.
- Ask yourself: Were it not for fear, what would I want to do to stop or prevent abuse of someone in our community? What can I do? What can we do?
- Given what each of us has learned about sexual abuse, no longer can any of us allow fear to keep us from working toward a safer community.
- Each of us has the unique opportunity to be the one (or among the many) who finally says and does something about making our community the best and safest place for children, families, and parents.
- Take some time now to talk about what you as an individual can do and what we as a group can do.

4. Divide the large group into small groups of eight. You may want to merge every other group from the previous activity into one large group. Provide each small group with a couple sheets of newsprint and a few markers. Instruct the small groups to develop a plan they can realistically support and can carry out in their efforts to keep young people safe. Be sure to do the following:

- Remind the participants that they have seen their work from other sessions promoted, advertised, and printed in various ways to get the word out to others who have not been a part of this awareness program.
- Assure the participants that you and the parish or school staff want to take their concerns and ideas seriously and that you hope to be able to support and accommodate the needs and creative ideas they have.
- Remind the groups to be realistic. No plan is too small; very simple efforts can make a big difference.
- Tell the groups they will be asked to show and explain to the other groups what they have created.
- Ask the participants whether they have any questions. If so, respond. If not, invite the groups to begin.
- Be sure to visit each small group to encourage them in their work and to answer any questions they might have. If your speaker is willing, ask him or her to visit groups and to add suggestions and comments where appropriate. If you decide it would be helpful to the participants, provide them with copies of the current bulletin or calendar so they will know about the programs and activities that are already happening in the community. Ask them to think about how those programs and activities could be improved by some awareness and support of child abuse prevention efforts.

5. After 10 minutes, tell the participants they should consider answering the following question as they begin to develop their plan more fully:

- How would this plan be implemented in our community?
- Where would we need to go to find resources?
- Whom would we seek out to help us?
- What can each member of our small group contribute to this plan or idea?
- Are there any obstacles to this plan? If so, how can we overcome them?

Allow an additional 10 minutes for the participants to consider the questions.

6. Gather the participants back into a large group. Ask each small group to present its ideas to the large group. When appropriate, make note of participants who show a strong interest in their personal efforts toward making these plans happen. Be sure to include those people in your next action steps for the community.

7. Invite a few of the participants to respond in the large group to the following questions:

- What positive efforts is our faith community already implementing that promote a safe and sacred environment?
- What do you think our community is missing or could improve on in regard to prevention and awareness?
- What would you like to see happen to improve the quality of safety and sanctity in our faith community?

8. Thank the participants for their courageous effort, and encourage them to consider how they can take part in keeping safety a number-one priority in the community.

Believing in the Power of Community (5 minutes)

1. Tell the group that the work they have accomplished thus far is valuable. Thank them for choosing to walk the journey of awareness together, and invite them to continue on the path to healing, protection, and hope. Offer any additional summary comments or thoughts. If you will be providing the participants with additional training or an educational session, this would be a good time to let them know what is available.

2. Distribute handout 8 and invite participants to recite the pledge together. (Note: The pledge is done in an antiphonal style, so you will have to divide the large group into side A and side B.)

Suggested Speaker Notes (2)

Thank you for taking the time to meet with our faith community to share some important information about preventing child sexual abuse and keeping our community safe and sacred. Each of our participants has completed age-appropriate learning sessions about child sexual abuse prior to the upcoming intergenerational gathering. We hope you will be able to support our efforts and share with us information about the services and support that are available to church members in order to prevent abuse and to reach out in times of crisis. A suggested outline for your presentation is provided below. Please plan for a 15- to 20-minute presentation with a few minutes following for questions and answers.

- Describe the history of abuse prevention in parishes, schools, the diocese, and Church Tradition.
- Describe the improvements that have been made in the effort to protect children in the Catholic Church faith community. These improvements may include struggles with, concerns about, and obstacles to safety.
- Highlight what a person can expect if he or she brings a concern regarding abuse in the community to the attention of a church leader or official or diocesan representative.
- Describe the Church's hopes for children. How do the faith community's leaders hope to provide safe and sacred places for the entire community?

At the conclusion of your presentation, please stay to hear the discussion and the ideas and questions that the group raises about how they would like to promote their commitment to safety and sanctity for the sake of our young community members.

Community Pledge

All. We believe in the power of community. We have the power to help, to heal, to prevent, and to protect.

Side A. We have the power to build one another up

Side B. and the power to destroy.

All. We choose to build.

Side A. We have the power to create safe places

Side B. and the power to take away self-confidence.

All. We choose to create.

Side A. We have the power to believe in the potential of one another

Side B. and the power to deny one another's right to safety.

All. We choose to believe.

All. We pledge to protect and heal one another. Our voices speak of our desire to love and be loved.

Side A. We are voices of hope,

Side B. voices of promise,

Side A. voices of peace,

Side B. voices of trust,

Side A. voices of safety,

Side B. voices of forgiveness,

Side A. voices of integrity,

Side B. voices of concern,

Side A. voices of belief,

Side B. voices of faith.

All. We know that our courage, our desire, and our motivation come from God. We ask God's help in obtaining our goal in being instruments of peace and healing. Amen.

Part C

RESOURCES FOR PARISH AND SCHOOL STAFF

Considerations in Ministry Planning

All adults who work with children and or young people must be capable of exercising good judgment and wisdom in their ministry. We recommend that you consider the following questions when planning any activity involving children or young people within the faith community:

- Who are the volunteers, and what is their training? Can or should additional training be offered?
- What is expected of the volunteers? How are those expectations communicated? What are the consequences of unmet expectations?
- What is expected of the young people who participate? How will those expectations be communicated? What are the consequences if those expectations are not met?
- How visible are the programs and activities? Do they involve a wide range of participants? Does the larger community know what programs and activities are available, who is involved in them, and how they affect the young people of the community?
- What opportunities are available for parents and other adults to be directly involved?
- What kind of programming is planned to teach critical thinking and to give young people the tools to mature into healthy adults?

Sample Parish Statement for Those Working with Young People

The community and pastoral staff of ________________ are committed to providing a safe environment to help young people learn to love and follow Jesus Christ. The disturbing and traumatic occurrence and recognition of physical and sexual abuse of children have claimed the attention of our nation, our society, and this community. Catholic schools and churches with programs for children are not insulated from those who abuse.

This community believes that it is vitally important to take decisive steps to ensure that all ministries are safe and provide a joyful experience for young people. The following policies reflect our commitment to provide protective care for all young people when they attend parish- or school-sponsored programs and activities:

- Volunteers who work with young people must be active members of the community for a minimum of six months and must be approved by appropriate parish or school personnel before they can begin working directly with young people in parish- or school-sponsored programs and activities.

- Potential volunteers must provide references that appropriate personnel or staff must verify.
- All ministry volunteers must observe the "two-person rule," avoiding one-on-one situations with young people whenever possible.
- Adult survivors of childhood physical or sexual abuse need the love and acceptance of this parish family.
- Individuals who have committed physical or sexual abuse, whether or not convicted, cannot work in any parish- or school-sponsored program, activity, or ministry involving young people.
- Opportunities for training in the prevention and recognition of abuse of young people will be provided by the various ministry areas of the parish or school. All volunteers and staff members who minister to and with young people must participate in such training.
- Volunteers and staff members must report to the pastor or administration any behaviors or incidents that seem abusive or inappropriate. Upon notification, the pastor or administration will take appropriate action and report in compliance with diocesan guidelines and the civil laws of the county and state.
- The parish administration will provide guidelines for volunteers who work with young people.

Sample Code of Conduct

This code of conduct shall be agreed upon and followed by all clergy, staff members, and volunteers who minister to and with young people. Your review and subsequent signature indicate your willingness and agreement to abide by the following guidelines:

- Only priests, seminarians, or their immediate family members may be overnight guests in rectories.
- Providing a young person with an alcoholic beverage, tobacco, or drugs is prohibited.
- Touching must be age-appropriate and based on the need of the young person and not on the need of the adult. An adult must avoid physical contact when alone with a young person. If a minor initiates physical contact, such as a hug, an appropriate, limited response is proper.
- Engaging in physical discipline of a young person is unacceptable. Discipline problems are to be directed and handled in coordination with parish or school staff and administration or the parents of the young person.
- Adults should not be alone with a young person in a residence, sleeping facility, locker room, rest room, dressing facility, or other closed room or isolated area that is inappropriate to a ministry relationship.

- Taking an overnight trip alone with a young person from the parish or school community who is not a member of your immediate family is prohibited.
- Sleeping in the same bed with a young person is prohibited. If attending a parish- or school-sponsored event that requires a stay in a hotel or other sleeping room with a group of young people, the adult must sleep in his or her own bed, using a roll-away or cot if necessary.
- Topics, vocabulary, recordings, films, games, computer software, or any other form of personal interaction or entertainment that could not be used comfortably in the presence of parents must not be used with young people. Sexually explicit or pornographic material is prohibited.
- Administering medication of any kind without written parental permission and parish or school staff approval is prohibited.
- If inappropriate personal or physical attraction develops between an adult and a young person, the adult is responsible to maintain clear professional boundaries.
- If one-on-one pastoral care of a young person should be necessary, avoid meeting in isolated environments. Schedule meetings at times and use locations that create accountability. Limit both the length and number of sessions, and make appropriate referrals. Notify parents of the meetings.
- Young people are not allowed to have keys to church facilities. If a young person has a key as a result of being a parish employee or volunteer, he or she should be properly screened.
- Driving a church or school vehicle is prohibited unless prior authorization has been received and the appropriate license or certification has been obtained.
- Permitting young people to cross a road by themselves while they are in your custodial care is prohibited.
- Taking photographs of young people while they are unclothed or dressing (e.g., in a locker room or bathing facility) is prohibited.
- If anyone (adult or minor) abuses a young person in your presence, immediately take appropriate steps to intervene and to provide a safe environment for the young person. Report the misconduct.
- No person may serve with young people or other protected persons if he or she has ever been convicted of any disqualifying offense, has ever been on probation, has ever received deferred adjudication for any disqualifying offense, or is presently pending any criminal charges for any disqualifying offense, until a determination of guilt or innocence is made, including any person who is presently on deferred adjudication. Disqualifying offenses include these:
  - **A felony classified as an offense against a person or family or involvement in an offense against a person or family.** Offenses

against a person include, but are not limited to, murder, assault, sexual assault, and abandoning or endangering a child. Offenses against a family include, but are not limited to, bigamy, incest, interfering with child custody, enticing a child, and harboring a runaway child.

- **A felony classified as an offense against public order or indecency.** Offenses against public order or indecency include, but are not limited to, prostitution, obscenity, and sexual performance by a child, possession or promotion of child pornography, and disorderly conduct.
- **A felony violation of any law intended to control the possession or distribution of any substance included as a controlled substance in the Texas Controlled Substance Act.**
- **A misdemeanor classified as sexual assault, indecency with a child, injury to a child, abandoning or endangering a child, sexual performance by a child, possession or promoting child pornography, enticing a child, bigamy, or incest.**

(Adapted from Catholic Diocese of Dallas, "Behavioral Guidelines for Working with Children or Youth")

Questions (and Commentary) for Screening Volunteers Who Work with Young People

The following questions may be helpful in evaluating the appropriateness of volunteers who will work with young people at your parish or school. The commentary that follows each question provides reasons for the type of question used.

1. How long have you lived in this community?
- *Long-term residents usually have community connections and commitments. Short-term residents should give you the opportunity to ask about their past experiences and relationships, including family relationships, jobs, and reasons for moving. It may be helpful to ask for references from people who have known the applicant for a long time.*

2. Why do you want to work with young people?
- *Does this person like young people? Does this person work well with children? Young people can sense if people really like them. For example, beware of someone who has an ax to grind regarding children and discipline. What is the applicant's motivation?*

3. Would your experience as a child have an impact on your working with children in this position?
   - *Look for body language and tone of voice. Be aware of anxiety about relationships with parents and siblings. Talk about current family relationships. Talk about childhood discipline and punishment. Will this person's ideas create conflict? Assess carefully (but do not necessarily exclude) someone who has experienced an abusive, dysfunctional childhood. Try to be sure this does not interfere with the person's ability to help others. Try to ascertain whether the applicant is trying to help himself or herself recover or whether he or she might project personal feelings on the children.*

4. How would your current relationships with family and friends impact your work with young people?
   - *Look for interpersonal relationships within the family—family stress, death, divorce, separation, and violent relationships. Beware of someone who doesn't have adult friends and who says, "Children are my best friends," or "I'd rather be with kids than adults."*

5. Has an issue or suspicion ever been raised that you may have abused, molested, or touched a child inappropriately? If so, how was it resolved?
   - *If an applicant answers yes, this person is a high risk! Be up front, and tell the applicant that for her or his own protection, as well as for the protection of the young people, volunteering to work with adults is much safer. If an applicant has abused a child in any way, she or he should never be allowed to work with young people.*

Recommended Resources

Organizations and Web Sites

Catholic Charities USA
www.catholiccharitiesusa.org
Catholic Charities USA promotes innovative strategies to address human needs and social injustice.

Center for Assault Prevention (CAP)
www.ncap.org
CAP's mission is to prevent interpersonal violence through curriculum development, research, and evaluation; public education; and comprehensive training.

Center for the Prevention of Sexual and Domestic Violence
www.cpsdv.org
This organization has a number of resources to help religious leaders and communities understand the religious issues associated with sexual abuse and domestic violence.

Childhelp USA
www.childhelpusa.org
The Childhelp USA National Child Abuse Hotline is a valuable resource for troubled parents, children in the midst of abuse, individuals requesting child abuse information, and professionals who need to make referrals to agencies.

Generation Five
www.generationfive.org
Generation 5 provides leadership training to community members, activists, and agency professionals and fosters national strategy and information exchange on child sexual abuse.

Justice for Children (JFC)
www.jfcadvocacy.org/index.stm
JFC is a national organization of citizens concerned about children's rights and protection from abuse.

The Linkup—Survivors of Clergy Abuse
www.thelinkup.org
This organization is dedicated to fighting for justice, preventing abuse, and helping victims heal.

MaleSurvivor
www.malesurvivor.org
MaleSurvivor conducts research, education, advocacy, and activism to promote prevention, treatment, and elimination of sexual abuse of male children and adults.

The National Call to Action (NCTA)
www.nationalcalltoaction.com
NCTA is a coalition of organizations and individuals dedicated to ensure that children flourish free from abuse and neglect.

National Center for Missing and Exploited Children (NCMEC)
www.cybertipline.com
NCMEC's CyberTipline is a toll-free line to report any information pertaining to the sexual exploitation of children on the Internet or in any industry that makes use of child pornography.

The National Children's Advocacy Center (NCAC)
www.ncac-hsv.org
NCAC provides prevention, intervention, and treatment services to physically and sexually abused children and their families through a child-focused, team approach.

National District Attorneys Association (NDAA)
www.ndaa-apri.org
Responding to an increasing volume of reported child abuse, the National District Attorneys Association serves as a central resource for training, expert legal assistance, court reform, and state-of-the-art information on criminal child abuse investigations and prosecutions.

National Federation for Catholic Youth Ministry (NFCYM)
www.nfcym.org
NFCYM has developed a number of resources to assist parishes, schools, and dioceses in addressing the topic of sexual abuse.

Parents Anonymous
www.parentsanonymous.org
This national organization encourages all parents to ask for help early, whatever the circumstances, to break the cycle of child abuse.

Prevent Child Abuse America (PCA America)
www.preventchildabuse.org
PCA America is a national, volunteer-based organization committed to preventing child abuse, in all its forms, through research, public education, and advocacy.

Rape, Abuse, & Incest National Network (RAINN)
www.rainn.org
RAINN operates a national hotline for victims of sexual assault. The hotline offers free, confidential counseling and support, twenty-four hours a day, from anywhere in the country.

The Safer Society Foundation, Inc. (SSFI)
www.safersociety.org
SSFI is a national research, advocacy, and referral center dedicated to the prevention and treatment of sexual abuse. SSFI offers a variety of services, including sex offender treatment referrals, responses to research requests, training, and consultation.

***STOP IT* NOW!**
www.stopitnow.org
STOP IT NOW! challenges abusers and people at risk of abusing to stop abusive behavior and to reach out for help. This organization educates adults about the ways to prevent child sexual abuse and promotes policy changes at the local and national level to support primary and secondary prevention strategies.

United States Conference of Catholic Bishops
Restoring Trust: Response to Clergy Sexual Abuse
www.usccb.org/comm/restoretrust.htm
This site includes statements from the United States bishops, the full text of the 2002 charter, as well as various articles, documents, and information relating to the Church's response to clerical abuse.

Voices in Action, Inc. (VOICES)
www.voices-action.org
VOICES helps victims of incest and child sexual abuse become survivors and generates public awareness of the prevalence of incest, its impact, and ways in which it can be prevented or stopped through educational programs.

Educational and Training Videos

Better Safe Than Sorry. Filmfair Communications. 1983. 15 minutes. Designed for a young age-group. Children are led through a discussion of three rules to help prevent sexual abuse. Potentially dangerous situations are dramatized to allow the children to decide how to react. Call 818-985-0244.

The Healing Years: A Documentary About Surviving Incest and Child Sexual Abuse. Center for the Prevention of Sexual Abuse and Domestic Violence. 1999. 52 minutes. Profiles three women through their journey of pain and despair from incest and their process of recovery as they work to end the cycle of incest and child sexual abuse for generations ahead. Religious issues are addressed in the study guide. Call 206-634-1903, or visit *www.cpsdv.org.*

Love—All That and More. Center for the Prevention of Sexual Abuse and Domestic Violence. Approximately 20 minutes for each video. This video series informs young people about the elements that make up healthy relationships and increases awareness and understanding about abuse. Call 206-634-1903, or visit *www.cpsdv.org.*

A Sacred Trust: Boundary Issues for Clergy and Spiritual Teachers. Center for the Prevention of Sexual Abuse and Domestic Violence. Approximately 22 minutes per video. This video series, designed for clergy and seminarians, consists of four training videos and a comprehensive facilitator's guide with background information, discussion questions, and suggestions for role-plays and other interactive activities. Call 206-634-1903, or visit *www.cpsdv.org.*

Print Resources

Burkett, Elinor, and Frank Bruni. *A Gospel of Shame: Children, Sexual Abuse, and the Catholic Church.* New York: Viking, 1993.

Colao, Flora, and Tamar Hosansky. *Your Children Should Know: Personal Safety Strategies for Parents to Teach Their Children.* New York: Harper and Row, 1987.

Cozzens, Donald B. *The Changing Face of the Priesthood: A Reflection on the Priest's Crisis of Soul.* Collegeville, MN: Liturgical Press, 2000.

Mather, Cynthia L. *How Long Does It Hurt? A Guide to Recovering from Incest and Sexual Abuse for Teenagers, Their Friends, and Their Families.* San Francisco: Jossey Bass, 1994.

McCarty, Robert J. *Protecting Young People: Our Sacred Trust.* Washington, DC: National Federation for Catholic Youth Ministry, 2002.

Plante, Thomas G., ed. *Bless Me Father for I Have Sinned: Perspectives on Sexual Abuse Committed by Roman Catholic Priests.* Westport, CT: Praeger, 1999.

Plummer, Carol. *Preventing Sexual Abuse: Activities and Strategies for Those Working with Children and Adolescents.* Holes Beach, FL: Learning Publications, 1997.

Rossetti, Stephen J. *Slayer of the Soul: Child Sexual Abuse in the Catholic Church.* Mystic, CT: Twenty-Third Publications, 1991.

________. *A Tragic Grace: The Catholic Church and Child Sexual Abuse.* Collegeville, MN: Liturgical Press, 1996.

United States Conference of Catholic Bishops (USCCB). *Restoring Trust: A Pastoral Response to Sexual Abuse.* Washington, DC: USCCB, 2002.

A Prayer Service of Reconciliation and Rededication

Setting the Prayer Environment

You will want to ensure that the gathering space provides an atmosphere of comfort, safety, and trust. You might hold the gathering at night, perhaps after the final session, with parents, young people, and staff present. If using the church building, be sure the sanctuary is barren—dimly lit, stripped of all altar clothes, candles, flowers, and so forth. In addition, you will need an outside area for one of the ritual activities.

Leadership Roles

You will need to assign a variety of roles for this prayer service to run smoothly and effectively:

- You will need an overall prayer coordinator to oversee planning and preparations, to gather needed materials and supplies, and to coordinate during the prayer service. Having someone take on this role will ensure that any unforeseen glitches can and will be addressed during the service.

- Two presiders are recommended for this service. The presiders should be laypeople rather than members of the clergy. Consider inviting two ministry leaders, or a young person and a ministry leader, to serve as the prayer service presiders. Both genders should be represented in the service leadership. The role of the presiders is to offer prayer and lead the participants in each of the prayer movements.
- A music leader should be available and should choose the music selections ahead of time. She or he should prepare a worship aid if you choose to use one.
- You will need someone to set up and assist with the lighting of the fire.
- You will need a young person to bring to the altar the water basin and branches.
- You will need a lector or cantor to proclaim or sing the Psalm response.
- You will need a parent and a child to bring to the altar the pitchers of water.
- You will need a family to bring forth the altar cloth, candles, flowers, and other decor.

Preparation

Gather the following items:

- ☐ torn fabric or cloth and straight pins
- ☐ flashlight
- ☐ self-stick notes, one for each participant
- ☐ pens or pencils, one for each participant
- ☐ vigil candles, one for each participant
- ☐ Paschal candle (Easter candle)
- ☐ a large water basin and a branch
- ☐ two large pitchers of water (in clear containers so the water is visible)
- ☐ metal basin or grill to burn small slips of paper (Be sure it is safe and containable.)
- ☐ charcoal and matches
- ☐ hymnals or worship aids with printed music, one for each participant
- ☐ copies of handout 8, "Community Pledge," one for each participant (You may also include the pledge in the worship aid if you create one.)

- Select various excerpts from "One Survivor's Story," in part A, chapter 3, of this manual. Choose excerpts you deem appropriate for the community gathered. Be sure to choose a few excerpts that reflect the hope and healing of the survivor.

- Set up the vigil candles, Paschal candle, charcoal, and metal basin or grill in a gathering space outside.
- Place the water basin, branch, pitchers of water, altar cloth, candles, and flowers on a small table at the back of the church.
- Select music accordingly. Possible selections might include these:
  - "Canticle of the Turning," by Rory Cooney, in *Gather Comprehensive* (Chicago: GIA Publications)
  - "Christ, Be Our Light," by Bernadette Farrell, in *Today's Missal Music Issue* (Portland, OR: Oregon Catholic Press)
  - "Confitemini Domino / Come and Fill," by Jacques Berthier / Taizé Community, in *Gather Comprehensive* (Chicago: GIA Publications)
  - "God of Day and God of Darkness," by Marty Haugen, in *Gather Comprehensive* (Chicago: GIA Publications)
  - "Jesus, Heal Us," by David Haas, in *Gather Comprehensive* (Chicago: GIA Publications)
  - "Remember Your Love," by D. Ducote, G. Daigle, and M. Balhoff, in *Today's Missal Music Issue* (Portland, OR: Oregon Catholic Press)

Procedure

1. As the participants enter the prayer space, invite each person to take a piece of torn fabric or cloth and pin it onto his or her shirt. Let them know that wearing a piece of torn fabric is a sign of loss and grief in the traditional Jewish ritual. Having the participants carry on that tradition is a sign of their current grief and loss at this time in the Church's history. Also provide each participant with a self-stick note and a pen or pencil.

2. Begin the service with the following prayer:
Leader: In the name of the Father and of the Son and of the Holy Spirit. The Lord be with you.
All: And also with you.

3. Invite the assembly to take a seat and spend a few moments in quiet prayer and reflection. You may wish to have the music leader play some quiet instrumental music during this time.

4. After a few minutes, invite the assembly to take a few additional moments to think about and reflect on how the images of God, Church, clergy, and community have been shattered, lost, questioned, or destroyed in light of the sexual abuse scandal and crisis. Allow a few moments for reflection. Then ask the assembly to write down one of those images. For example, one participant might write, "A sense of trust in the Church has been lost." If you find that participants are having difficulty writing down an image, offer a few examples from your own life.

5. Ask the assembly to stand and follow a procession to the outdoor area where you have placed the metal basin or grill. Be sure they bring their self-stick notes with them. Ask them to process in silence.

6. Once all have gathered around the metal basin or grill, ask for silence once again. Invite the participants to pause to listen to the sounds of the night. Then offer the following prayer. (Here is where the flashlight will come in handy.)

> Gracious and loving Creator, you once hovered over the chaos and darkness of the universe and breathed into it your life and beauty. We pray once again that you come and breathe into our chaos, our darkness.
>
> Come, loving God, to your world, your faith community, your shepherds, your people gathered in your name this night.
>
> Heal your peoples' wounds, and listen to these cries and lamentations as we pray most especially for the victims of sexual abuse in our society and in our Church. Let their pain and suffering be ever before us as we rededicate ourselves to the protection of young people everywhere and, most especially, in this community of faith. We pray together in the name of the Lord. Amen.

7. Request that the fire be lit. You may wish to invite the participants to join in song while the lighting is taking place.

8. Once the fire has been lit and is secure, invite the participants to tear their self-stick notes and place them on the fire. When all the participants have discarded their self-stick notes, light the Paschal candle and then offer each participant a vigil candle to light from the Paschal candle.

9. Invite the music leader to begin a procession back into the church as the participants join in singing the penitential rite ("Lord, have mercy" or "Kyrie").

10. Once all have gathered and are seated in the church, ask the young person you have chosen to come forward and place the water basin and branch on the barren altar. Invite the participants to stand in silence as this occurs. Then offer the following prayer as the lights are turned on and the candles are extinguished:

> Loving God, your people are gathered in the light and hope of your love. Gather us in this night as we dedicate ourselves to protecting the innocent among us. Helps us heal our shattered dreams and hopes. Your love and grace will guide us in our journey. Be with us, we pray! Consecrate us to your vision. May the light we bear in our

hands become the light of understanding in our minds and the wisdom of words on our lips to protect your children always and everywhere. We pray in Jesus' name. Amen.

11. Invite the reader or cantor to come forward to proclaim Psalm 93 in spoken word or song. Allow a few moments of silence to follow.

12. In a prayerful manner, share with the assembly the excerpts you have chosen from "One Survivor's Story." Allow a few moments of reflection between excerpts. Then tie in your own reflections or comments by using one of the following Scripture passages:

- Luke 19 (Jesus' weeping with us this night)
- Luke 24:13–35 (lost hope, shattered expectations, being broken and poured forth in our sadness)
- Matthew 5:1–11 (children as our example of what the Lord desires)

13. Signal the selected parent and child to bring to the altar the pitchers of water and to pour the water quietly into the water basin. As this is happening, share the following point with the participants:

- With the sign of the cross and water from this bowl, we vow to work toward keeping all children safe, and we promise to offer our compassion and support to all those who have been harmed by the sin of sexual abuse.

As a sign of this commitment, the two presiders bless each other with the water.

14. While the music leader is directing the assembly in song, approach the assembly and bless the people and place of worship. At the same time, signal the chosen family to come forward to dress the altar with cloth, candles, and flowers.

15. Invite the assembly to stand and proclaim together the "Community Pledge." Then conclude the service by offering the following prayer:

> Most gracious and loving trinity,
> You have gathered us this night to be re-created in your image.
> Help us to see as you see! To speak as you speak! To touch as you touch!
> As we go forth this night, guide us, we pray.
> Be with us in our going forth and in our returning,
> In our sleeping and in our wakefulness,
> In our tears and in our hopes.
> Let us go then and do your bidding.
> Let us build your kingdom where you live forever and ever. Amen.

Acknowledgments

The scriptural quotations contained herein are from the New Revised Standard Version of the Bible, Catholic Edition. Copyright © 1993 and 1989 by the Division of Christian Education of the National Council of the Churches of Christ in the United States of America. All rights reserved.

The excerpts in this book marked *Catechism of the Catholic Church*, *Catechism*, or *CCC* are from the English translation of the *Catechism of the Catholic Church* for use in the United States of America. Copyright © 1994 by the United States Catholic Conference, Inc.—Libreria Editrice Vaticana. Used with permission.

The excerpt on page 9 is from the song "A Place at the Table," lyrics by Shirley Erena Murray, on the music CD *A Place at the Table,* by Lori True (Chicago: GIA Publications, 2002). Lyrics copyright © 1998 by Hope Publishing. CD copyright © 2002 by GIA Publications. Used with permission.

The principles on page 16 are from "The Five Principles to Follow in Dealing with Accusations of Sexual Abuse," by the United States Conference of Catholic Bishops (USCCB), at *www.usccb.org/comm/kit4.htm.* Accessed June 12, 2003. Copyright © June 3, 2003, by the USCCB. Permission applied for.

Portions of chapters 1 and 2 are adapted and based on the dissertation "Sexually Offending and Non-Offending Roman Catholic Priests: Characterization and Analysis," by Gerard J. McGlone, SJ, PhD. Copyright © 2001 by Gerard J. McGlone, SJ, PhD. Used with permission.

The excerpt on pages 23–24 is from "Essential Norms for Diocesan/ Eparchial Policies Dealing with Allegations of Sexual Abuse of Minors by Priests or Deacons," by the United States Conference of Catholic Bishops

(USCCB), at *www.usccb.org/bishops/norms.htm*. Accessed June 9, 2003. Copyright © June 2003 by the USCCB. The quotation within the excerpt is from *Canonical Delicts Involving Sexual Misconduct and Dismissal from the Clerical State,* by the USCCB (Washington, DC: USCCB, 1995), page 6. Copyright © 1995. Used with permission.

The statistics from Finkelhor and Rogers and Tremain, on pages 24–25, are quoted from Stop It Now!, at *www.stopitnow.org/comquest.html*. Accessed June 9, 2003. Copyright © 2000–2002 by Stop It Now! All rights reserved. Used with permission.

The statistic about male sexual offenders on page 25 is from "Sexual Abuse and Young Children," the Florida Center for Parent Involvement, at *www.fmhi.usf.edu/institute/pubs/pdf/cfs/fcpi/violence.htm*. Accessed June 23, 2003. Copyright © 1999 by the Florida Center for Parent Involvement, Louis de la Parte Florida Mental Health Institute, and University of South Florida, Tampa, Florida. All rights reserved.

The myths and facts on pages 26–27 are from "Myths and Facts About Sex Offenders," the Center for Sex Offender Management, at *www.csom.org/pubs/mythsfacts.html*. Accessed June 10, 2003. Office of Justice Programs, U. S. Department of Justice.

The statistics on page 32 are from "Online Victimization: A Report on the Nation's Youth," by the Crimes Against Children Research Center, at *www.missingkids.com/missingkids/servlet/ResourceServlet?LanguageCountry=enUS&PageId=869*. Accessed June 9, 2003. Copyright © 2000 by The National Center for Missing and Exploited Children. All rights reserved. Provided courtesy of Terri Dalaney, director of publications.

The excerpt on page 40 is from "A Catholic Response to Sexual Abuse: Confession, Contrition, Resolve," Bishop Wilton D. Gregory's presidential address on June 13, 2002, at *www.usccb.org/bishops/presidentialaddress.htm*. Accessed July 1, 2003. Copyright © June 3, 2003, by the United States Conference of Catholic Bishops. Permission applied for.

The statement on page 41 is from a press release titled "Bishop Gregory Stresses Force of Action on Child Sexual Abuse," at *www.usccb.org/comm/archives/2002/02-113.htm*. Accessed July 1, 2003. Copyright © June 3, 2003, United States Conference of Catholic Bishops. Permission applied for.

The behavioral guidelines on pages 142–144 are adapted from "Behavioral Guidelines for Working with Children or Youth," from the Catholic Diocese of Dallas, at *www.cathdal.org/SafeEnvironment.htm*. Accessed June 12, 2003. Permission applied for.

To view copyright terms and conditions for Internet materials cited here, log on to the home pages for the referenced Web sites.

During this book's preparation, all citations, facts, figures, names, addresses, telephone numbers, Internet URLs, and other information cited within were verified for accuracy. The authors and Saint Mary's Press staff have made every attempt to reference current and valid sources, but we cannot guarantee the content of any source, and we are not responsible for any changes that may have occurred since our verification. If you find an error in, or have a question or concern about, any of the information or sources listed within, please contact Saint Mary's Press.

Endnotes Cited in Quotations from the *Catechism of the Catholic Church*, Second Edition

1. *Heb* 5:1; cf. *Ex* 29:1–30; *Lev* 8
2. St. Gregory of Nazianzus, *Oratio* 2, 71, 74, 73: PG 35, 480–481
3. St. John Vianney, quoted in B. Nodet, *Jean-Marie Vianney, Curé d'Ars,* 100
4. Cf. CIC, cann. 290–293; 1336 § 1 3°, 5°; 1338 § 2; Council of Trent: DS 1774
5. Cf. CIC, cann. 290–293; 1336 § 1 3°, 5°; 1338 § 2; Council of Trent: DS 1774
6. Cf. CIC, cann. 290–293; 1336 § 1 3°, 5°; 1338 § 2; Council of Trent: DS 1774

School and catechetical leaders share the awesome responsibility of safeguarding the health and well-being of students whenever students are entrusted to their care. This entails ongoing training so that educators and catechists are familiar with any and all threats to student safety. *Creating Safe and Sacred Places: Identifying, Preventing, and Healing Sexual Abuse* is an outstanding resource that addresses a most insidious form of harm to children. The authors effectively portray the breadth and scope of sexual abuse and then provide a comprehensive training process to assist educators, catechists, and volunteers in acting promptly and appropriately when signs of abuse are present. This manual is a timely response to the United States Bishops' call to be proactive in dealing with all incidents of sexual abuse. It is an excellent resource that should be in the personal library of everyone who holds a leadership position in the Church's educational ministry.

Timothy Dwyer, assistant executive director, Chief Administrators of Catholic Education, National Catholic Educational Association

Youth ministry leaders in all settings will value *Creating Safe and Sacred Places.* This resource supports a proactive ministerial and pastoral response to the issues of sexual abuse, and the training sessions for leaders, parents, and young people are practical, clear, and easy to implement. The background information on sexual abuse, especially within the context of the Catholic Church, is very valuable, and the section providing resources to assist parishes and schools in developing policies and procedures is an additional and welcomed benefit.

Robert J. McCarty, executive director,
National Federation for Catholic Youth Ministry

Creating Safe and Sacred Places: Identifying, Preventing, and Healing Sexual Abuse is a very timely and user-friendly manual for all who minister to young people. Not only are terms clearly defined, guidelines carefully established, and resources amply documented, but also practical working sessions are provided for use with parents, teachers, administrators, youth ministers, and the young people themselves. McGlone, Shrader, and Delgatto provide a tool for education, prayer, discussion, and action in response to the topic of sexual abuse. *Creating Safe and Sacred Places* should find its way into all those faith-based communities that are committed to honestly addressing the issue and protecting our young people.

Jack Podsiadio, SJ, executive director,
Nativity Educational Centers Network

McGlone, Shrader, and Delgatto have gifted our troubled Church with the finest resource and guide available for dealing with the current crisis of sexual abuse. Most important, this is a handbook of prevention. The map the authors lay out is practical, accessible, and valuable to an entire parish family, from pastor to parent to child. Those who follow this program will certainly create safe places and help keep them sacred.

A. W. Richard Sipe, author of *Celibacy in Crisis: A Secret World Revisited*